KANYE WEST

Recent Titles in Greenwood Biographies

KANYE WEST

A Biography

Bob Schaller

GREENWOOD BIOGRAPHIES

GREENWOOD PRESS
An Imprint of ABC-CLIO, LLC

A B C • C L I O

Santa Barbara, California • Denver, Colorado • Oxford, England

Library of Congress Cataloging-in-Publication Data

Schaller, Bob.
   Kanye West : a biography / Bob Schaller.
     p. cm. — (Greenwood biographies)
   Includes bibliographical references and index.
   ISBN 978-0-313-37460-9 (hardcover : alk. paper) — ISBN 978-0-313-37461-6 (ebook)
  1. West, Kanye. 2. Rap musicians—United States—Biography. I. Title.
  ML420.W452S33 2009
  782.421649092—dc22
  [B]   2009016190

13 12 11 10 09   1 2 3 4 5

This book is also available on the World Wide Web as an eBook.
Visit www.abc-clio.com for details.

ABC-CLIO, LLC
130 Cremona Drive, P.O. Box 1911
Santa Barbara, California 93116-1911

This book is printed on acid-free paper ∞
Manufactured in the United States of America

CONTENTS

CONTENTS

Photo essay follows page 66

SERIES FOREWORD

In response to high school and public library needs, Greenwood developed this distinguished series of full-length biographies specifically for student use. Prepared by field experts and professionals, these engaging biographies are tailored for high school students who need challenging yet accessible biographies. Ideal for secondary school assignments, the length, format, and subject areas are designed to meet educators' requirements and students' interests.

Greenwood offers an extensive selection of biographies spanning all curriculum-related subject areas, including social studies, the sciences, literature and the arts, history, and politics, as well as popular culture, covering public figures and famous personalities from all time periods and backgrounds, both historic and contemporary, who have made an impact on American or world culture. Greenwood biographies were chosen based on comprehensive feedback from librarians and educators. Consideration was given to both curriculum relevance and inherent interest. The result is an intriguing mix of the well known and the unexpected, the saints and sinners from long-ago history and contemporary pop culture. Readers will find a wide array of subject choices from fascinating crime figures like Al Capone to inspiring pioneers like Margaret Mead, from the greatest minds of our time like Stephen Hawking to the most amazing success stories of our day like J. K. Rowling.

While the emphasis is on fact, not glorification, the books are meant to be fun to read. Each volume provides in-depth information about the subject's life from birth through childhood, the teen years, and adulthood.

A thorough account relates family background and education, traces personal and professional influences, and explores struggles, accomplishments, and contributions. A timeline highlights the most significant life events against a historical perspective. Bibliographies supplement the reference value of each volume.

ACKNOWLEDGMENTS

Thanks to my son, Garrett Paul Schaller, for turning me on to hip-hop; to Professor Shannon Bichard, PhD, at Texas Tech, for explaining celebrity branding to me; and to librarian Carrye Syma for research assistance. And my deep appreciation to super agent Bob Diforio and Greenwood editor George Butler for making me make myself a better, more patient, and more thorough writer.

INTRODUCTION

His name, his style, and the way he conducts his own business is unique. Yet Kanye West's upbringing is notably different from the pioneers of the hip-hop industry, and his wardrobe is more akin to something out of 90210 than a rap video.

So even when Kanye West (pronounced Con-yay, not Can-yee) calls himself one of a kind, he might be more accurate than even he himself realizes. In fact, his mother said that his first name, in Ethiopian, means "the only one,"[1] though others have claimed that is the name's meaning in Swahili. No matter, "one" is a familiar number to West. He has ascended to the top of the hip-hop charts, often battling head to head with established hip-hop heavyweights and always coming out on top when it comes to sales and hit singles. He started as a producer for the likes of Beanie Sigel, Alicia Keys, Ludacris, and Twista, and when he worked on Jay-Z's smash album *Blueprint*, Kanye West already had his own plans for a career as an artist.

Though he distanced himself from higher education as quickly as he could, against his mother's wishes, by dropping out of both the American Academy for the Arts and Chicago State University, he keeps his sense of humor about it, and his education is constantly part of his songs. His first three album titles were *The College Dropout*, *Late Registration*, and *Graduation*, all college-themed, and the little bear that appears on all three CD covers and his Web site, and which will likely be a big part of his brand-building and promotion, is affectionately referred to by Kanye as the "Dropout Bear." His charity work has included a big push through the foundation he created to keep minority students in school through junior high, high school, and college, and has done charitable events with hurricane victims, for environmental causes, and to help veterans of the war in Iraq who were having a hard time getting on their feet once they got back to the United States and tried to move forward with their lives.

Yet he is not, like a lot of hip-hop artists, from what might be called a rough upbringing. Indeed, West is articulate and thoughtful and does not subscribe to the various gang conflicts and hip-hop wars, which have included real bullets and resulted in some of the top stars of the craft being killed in their prime.

"I think I might have some problems with being accepted and just really fitting in because, you know . . . there is a lot of things that are different about me," West said. "I just don't fit into, like, the cookie cutter, you know . . . who you're supposed to be as a rapper or who you're supposed to be as a black man or who you're supposed to be as an entertainer, who you're supposed to be as a celebrity, you know? I don't, I don't just follow those rules."[2]

West's "rap sheet" has only lyrics, not felonies or misdemeanors. Yet West told Jamie Foxx in a Business Network interview that he has to be aware of the gang element in hip-hop.

"I'll only speak about it as lightly as possible, but the gangstas are a strong element in hip-hop that controls a lot of it," West said. "I definitely feel like I avoid a lot of problems because I am with Roc-A-Fella Records. But what's so crazy about the gangstas is they got star power and 'hood power at the same time."[3]

However, when it comes to demanding respect and commanding attention, West is in the spotlight, whether it is shining on him or not. He draws as much attention for his responses to real or perceived "disses" as he does for his top-selling songs, taking over the stage at awards shows when his nomination fails to reap the top prize. The media has a field day with Kanye's rants of self-righteousness, claiming he is stealing the attention from those who deserve it. But that's West's entire beef in a nutshell: he believes he is the one who deserves it, and he speaks out because of what he believes is the oversight, insincerity, and injustice of those who vote for the awards.

"I really believed in myself," West said. "And you know, I want to just apologize to everybody out there who says I'm arrogant. I apologize to everybody for believing in myself."[4]

He is as much MTV's artistic star as he is the music network's conscience and nemesis, calling out the network for exploiting stars who are struggling with personal and legal problems. He bites the hand that feeds him, in other words, and does not apologize because his comments come from deep-seated beliefs, not the spur-of-the-moment antics as described by some reporters. In addition to taking on the network that helped make him a star, he took on the president of the United States in the aftermath of Hurricane Katrina, using his platform to call attention to the plight of minorities and wondering aloud if the government would have offered such shoddy disaster-response measures if a community of white people had been the victims. He also took the unprecedented step of calling out the hip-hop community for its treatment of gays, a move requiring such verve and veracity that the expected icy response to West's call for tolerance and respect was muted.

West is as likely to be found on the cover of hip-hop magazines as he is GQ, his sense of fashion perhaps unparalleled not just in hip-hop, but in music at large. His Pastelle clothing line, which after years of delay is expected to be released in 2009, will bring colors not familiar to hip-hop, yet the line has even been worn by fellow rappers for photo shoots. Kanye is a showman much in the tradition of Elton John, or even Liberace, but unlike other diamond wearers, West has a social conscience that belies his flashy bling, even calling attention to the diamond trade that kills and exploits people in areas of the world many of his listeners could not find on a globe.

Kanye's big breakthrough as a producer, which put him with Roc-A-Fella/Def Jam's elite, was Jay-Z's album *Blueprint*. Four of Jay-Z's songs were produced by Kanye, including the top 10 Billboard hit "Izzo," which rose to number 8. Though in the song "Takeover," which Kanye produced and co-wrote, Jay-Z slammed Nas and Mobb Deep, with whom he was feuding at the time, Kanye ended up working with both of them, and he and Nas became particularly close, all while Kanye continued to be a sort of little brother to Jay-Z. Kanye has done nothing to feud with other rappers, and even while preparing do a release-date battle with 50 Cent, he offered praise to Fiddy's work and said he continued to be a fan of, and to even look up to, 50 Cent.

Equal parts Bob Dylan as a social protestor and Tupac or Biggie as a hip-hop innovator—and so involved and educated in fashion that he not only writes a fashion column for a magazine but also is teaming with a top designer to bring out his own line of shoes, with plans in place for a line of women's wear—the mercurial West is on the cusp of becoming one of the most influential entertainers of his generation. A talented producer, West as an artist shot to the top of the charts from the day he cut his first album, and his popularity has "touched the sky" ever since. Still, wherever he goes, whatever he does, he is the center of controversy in one form or another, and even "Touch the Sky" brought legal maneuvers from a previous generation's most outspoken daredevil, an issue resolved amicably.

NOTES

1. Donda West. *Raising Kanye: Life Lessons from the Mother of a Hip-Hop Superstar*. New York: Pocket Books, 2007.

2. Terry Moran. "Home with Kanye West." *Nightline*, ABC, September 24, 2007.

3. Jamie Foxx. "Kanye West." *Interview*, August 2004.

4. Kimberly Davis. "Kanye West: Hip-Hop's New Big Shot." *Ebony*, April 2005.

TIMELINE: EVENTS IN THE LIFE OF KANYE WEST

June 8, 1977	Kanye Omari West is born in Atlanta, Georgia, to Donda and Ray West.
1980	Kanye moves to Chicago with his mother after Donda and Ray divorce. Kanye continues to visit his father, who soon moves from Atlanta to Maryland.
1987–1988	Donda takes Kanye to China for a school year as part of her academic career in an exchange program.
1996–1998	Kanye drops out of the American Academy of Art and Chicago State University.
2000–2001	Kanye produces two songs for Jay-Z's album *Blueprint*.
October 23, 2002	Kanye falls asleep at the wheel and breaks his jaw in a car accident that would inspire "Through the Wire," the song he wrote and recorded with his jaw wired shut.
February 10, 2004	Kanye releases his first album, *The College Dropout*.
August 22, 2005	On MTV's special "All Eyes on Kanye West," Kanye speaks out against homophobia in hip-hop.
September 2, 2005	During an NBC fundraiser for victims of Hurricane Katrina, Kanye says on national TV, "George Bush doesn't care about black people."

August 30, 2005	Kanye releases his second album, *Late Registration*.
Early August 2006	Kanye proposes to girlfriend Alexis Phifer.
November 2, 2006	West storms the stage at the MTV-Europe awards when Justice and Simian are awarded best video. West claims "Touch the Sky" should have won.
November 7, 2006	While opening for U2 in Australia, West apologizes for the November 2 incident.
December 2006	Daredevil Evel Knievel sues West for using his likeness and image in Kanye's video for "Touch the Sky."
September 11, 2007	West's third album, *Graduation*, is released on the same day—by West's choosing—as 50 Cent's new album, and it outsells 50 Cent by more than a quarter-million copies.
November 10, 2007	Donda West dies from complications related to cosmetic surgery.
Late November 2007	Less than a week before Knievel's death, Evel Knievel and Kanye West settle their differences when Kayne personally visits Knievel's home. The lawsuit is settled, and they pose for what would be the last known pictures of Evel's life.
January 10, 2008	The Los Angeles County Coroner's Office releases its final autopsy that reports Donda West died of coronary heart disease and multiple postoperative factors related to cosmetic surgery.
February 10, 2008	Kanye wins four Grammy awards and performs a special version of "Hey Mama" in a tribute to his mother, Donda, who died three months earlier to the day.
April 21, 2008	Various news outlets confirm that Kanye and Alexis Phifer have broken off their engagement and are no longer together.
May 16, 2008	MTV names Kanye the year's "Number 1 MC in the Game."
August 2008	Kanye announces plans to open a series of "Fatburger" restaurants in Chicago.

Chapter 1

HUMBLE BEGINNINGS

Though Kanye West is often correctly associated with his longtime hometown of Chicago, he actually was born in Atlanta, Georgia.

Kanye's parents married in 1974, three years before he was born.[1] And Kanye spent the first three years of his life in Atlanta until his parents divorced. His father was a photographer for the *Atlanta Journal-Constitution* newspaper and also completed graduate school. Ray West has expressed creative talent through his photography, which in addition to the newspaper work included freelance photography through his own business. Ray West also has entrepreneurial interests and has opened several businesses, including a retail water outlet as well as his photography store.[2]

The metro Atlanta area, including the suburbs, has more than five million people, and from 2000 to 2006, it grew by more than 20 percent, which gave it the designation of fastest-growing metro area in the country. The city continues to earn praise and distinction from such organizations as the government's Environmental Protection Agency for its "green" or ecofriendly practices.

Atlanta's history is deep and rich, arguably as notable a U.S. city that has ever existed and certainly one of the most significant Southern metro areas in the country's history. In one of America's more shameful civil rights moments, in 1836 Cherokee Indians were removed from the area so that the Western and Atlanta Railroad could be built to provide trade with the Midwest. With a half-dozen buildings in 1842, the area was named Marthasville. A railroad executive pushed for the area to be renamed Atlantica-Pacifica, which was soon after shortened to Atlanta, and the city was incorporated by its new name on December 29, 1847.

THE SPIRIT OF ATLANTA

Atlanta became part of America's conscience during the Civil War. As a major trade hub with complete rail lines, Atlanta had great strategic value. After several bloody battles that resulted in the city being under a four-month siege by Union troops, the Confederate Army evacuated the city. The mayor surrendered, and Union general William Sherman ordered "Confederate assets"—which meant everything connected to the business and military interest of the South, so in effect, everything—to be destroyed. Two months later, Sherman ordered the city, with the exception of hospitals and churches, burned to the ground.

After the war, with slaves freed, the U.S. Army kept troops nearby to supervise the reconstruction of Atlanta, which included two black schools as part of Atlanta's public school system. The charter for Atlanta University, where Donda West would get her master's degree just over a century later, was launched in 1867, making Atlanta University the first of several notable black colleges in the area. Relying more on business than its traditional base of agriculture (which was still a very significant part of the economy), Atlanta became the state's capital and was advertised as the "New South" to draw investors.

As the century turned, so turned up more racial conflict for Atlanta. In 1906 the Atlanta Race Riot left nearly 30 dead.

When *Gone with the Wind*, a classic movie set during the Civil War that also included the city's burning, premiered in 1939 in Atlanta, not only were the film's stars Clark Gable and Vivien Leigh in attendance, but singing in a boys' choir was also a young man named Martin Luther King Jr., who was part of the congregation attending the premiere from the Ebenezer Baptist Church, where his father, Martin Luther King Sr., ministered.

Martin Luther King Jr. was born Michael King Jr. His father, Reverend Michael King Sr., took his wife and children, including then five-year-old Michael Jr., to Germany, where he was so moved by the accounts of German Protestant Martin Luther that upon returning to America, Michael King changed his own name to Martin Luther King Sr. and his son's name to Martin Luther King Jr.

Of course, Martin Luther King Jr. went onto become one of the most important civil rights leaders in American history before he was assassinated in Memphis on April 4, 1968. He was posthumously awarded the Presidential Medal of Freedom in 1977, and a national holiday in his honor was declared in 1986.

The city would go on to host the Olympics in 1996, which were a poster for well-run Olympics until an anti-abortion fanatic, Eric Rudolph, who, like Oklahoma City bomber Timothy McVeigh, had served in the U.S. Army, bombed the Centennial Olympic Park, an event captured on network television as American swimmer Janet Evans was being interviewed. The blast killed one and injured 111. So Atlanta is one of America's flagship Southern cities, for memorable moments and even atrocities that shaped the nation into what it is today.

LEAVING ATLANTA FOR THE MIDWEST

Even in day care, Kanye was a sort of ringleader.[3] Kids would just naturally seem to gravitate toward him as he entertained them and kept a running dialogue with himself. Yet he didn't lead in the traditional way—when those following him expected him to go left, he went right. And when everyone got used to going right, he'd go left. He liked to both entertain people and test them too, even as a small child. His mother remembered a little boy who was not insubordinate but who did need to be reined in at times.

She had a philosophy that keeping Kanye's mind on the right track was important, but she also allowed for a lot of creativity for her son. She wanted to see him blossom into what he wanted to, and could, become, not just what she wanted him to do.

His mother remembered that as a child, Kanye was always using his imagination and had great critical thinking skills. He was, she said in interviews, verbal before he could speak, as if the words were so eager to jump out of his mouth that they could not wait to be formed properly. He was clearly a thinker and had a lot to say.[4]

After his mother went on a prestigious academic Fulbright Scholar trip to conduct research with other scholars in India for nine weeks during her first year in Chicago, when Kanye was still 3 years old, she returned home promising never to leave her pride and joy, Kanye, for such a length of time ever again.[5]

This time as a three-year-old was important in Kanye's life—it also involved his parents' divorce and Donda West's move from Atlanta to Chicago. Donda was taking herself and her son to a major metropolitan city with no friends and family in the area. Yet because she had a good job, she was able to buy a good house in a nice neighborhood. Donda made the move so that she could teach college English at an urban school, Chicago State University.[6]

Chicago State University was a great playground for young Kanye's mind as he tagged along with his mother after hours or sometimes even during her own office hours at work. The school is a community unto itself, its campus basically a small town of sorts, with mostly bright young people and well-educated faculty, certainly a stimulating environment with largely goal-oriented and intelligent people. Kanye's after-school environment was this state university campus. With books everywhere, he could look to thoughtful, reflective people to have conversations with when his mother was busy with a student or faculty member, and there were safe hallways to stretch his legs, stairs to run up and down, and college students who got a kick out of Dr. West's young son and his high energy. So did his kindergarten teacher, who told Dr. West that her young son certainly had no problem whatsoever with self-esteem.[7]

After a year of renting the top apartment in a three-floor home their first year in Chicago, Donda bought a house in the suburb of South Shore.[8] Kanye and his mom had a nice backyard, were within walking distance of Lake Michigan's shore, enjoyed a cultured neighborhood, and were less than four miles from Chicago State University, which was just to the southwest on 95th Street.

The community was solidly middle-class, but had undergone a lot of strife in previous decades. Bordered by 67th Street to the north, 79th Street to the south, Lake Michigan to the east, and Stony Island Avenue to the west, the area had strong ties to the Illinois Central Railroad, which built the South Kenwood Station in 1881 on what is now 71st Street. The city of Chicago annexed the land in 1889, followed shortly by Chicago's historical World's Columbian Exposition in 1893; the fair was located nearby in Jackson Park, just 10 blocks north of what would become South Shore. The Fair drew builders to the area, who put up homes and businesses as the area boomed.

With the India experience in mind, when Donda was offered to be part of an exchange program with a university in Nanjing, China, she was going to turn it down, until those involved told her Kanye could certainly go along, and she knew he would be enriched by the cultural experience— and challenged to express himself in a country where he knew neither the language nor customs.

There were bumps on the trip—Kanye, though 10 years old, was put into a first-grade class because of language barriers.[9] He and his mother were basically the only black people in the region, and both believed by the way their Chinese neighbors stared that many had not seen black people before. But Kanye was an entertainer. He used to show off break-dancing for other kids and was such a must-see act that he occasionally made pocket change by charging kids when they'd plead for him to put on an exhibition. In later years, Kanye would perform as an opening act for rock bands for an audience that at first did not get him or have an interest in his genre, yet he would win those audiences over, just as he had those groups of students in China.[10] He also became functional with the language, smoothly learning the various inflections and terms that allowed him to not just get by, but communicate with people on a daily basis. The highlight of the trip, though, and the experience his mother would never forget, was their hike up Yellow Mountain.[11]

Kanye persuaded his mother to climb that mountain with him. Yellow Mountain is a part of the Huangshan range in the Anhui province. Kanye's mother wrote in her book, *Raising Kanye*, about how against her better judgment, she gave into then 10-year-old Kanye and hiked the mountain with him, and it's a memory neither would ever forget.

But the time in China also made Kanye know what it felt like to be the one odd person in the crowd. Though he does now and did then love attention, he would become uncomfortable with the staring when his mother was with him.[12] Certainly, Kanye's later insistence on tolerance in the hip-hop community was framed in no small part from his experience in China, though he did pick up a working knowledge of the language and seemed culturally enriched by the experience rather than scarred in any way.

The Chicago area in which Donda and Kanye resided became known as South Shore in the 1920s. The South Shore Country Club had guests such as famed pilot Amelia Earhart, actress Jean Harlow, and American legend Will Rogers. Between 1920 and 1930, South Shore grew from just under 32,000 residents to 79,000, and in 1940 the diverse culture was evidenced by the 15 Protestant churches, four Catholic churches, and four Jewish synagogues. In the 1950s, blacks started moving into South Shore, which a group of white citizens claimed concerned them—so much so that they formed the South Shore Commission in hopes of "managing integration," which sought to measure the decline of the community and racial balance. By 1970, 69 percent of South Shore residents were black, and by 1980, that number was 95 percent; one year later, the community included Donda and Kanye West. However, the area remained middle-class, had nice, well-kept homes and neighborhoods, and had no more measurable violent instances than other Chicago middle-class neighborhoods. With a cultural center and good schools, it was a far cry from the housing projects of Chicago where a lot of minorities were forced to live in crime and poverty.

The Jackson Heights development, on the north end of South Shore, has been home to Rev. Jesse Jackson and Bo Diddley, and as of 2008, it boasted television Judge James Mathis as a resident.

NOTES

1. Donda West. *Raising Kanye: Life Lessons from the Mother of a Hip-Hop Superstar*. New York: Pocket Books, 2007.

2. Greg Kot. "Rapper's Rise: From South Side to Top of the Charts." *Chicago Tribune*, February 11, 2004, http://www.rocafella.com/News.aspx?item=101084&sectionid=137.

3. Jenny Eliscu. "Genius Is as Genius Does." *USA Today Weekend*, August 19, 2007.

4. Donda West. *Raising Kanye*.

5. Nui Te Koha. "Kanye's New Sort of Rap." *(Australia) Sunday Mail*, September 16, 2007.

6. Donda West. *Raising Kanye*.

7. Greg Kot. "Rapper's Rise."

8. Donda West. *Raising Kanye*.

9. Ibid.

10. Ibid.

11. Greg Kot. "Rapper's Rise."

12. Donda West. *Raising Kanye*.

Chapter 2

KANYE'S FATHER

Although his father was no longer a day-to-day presence in Kanye's life after the move to Chicago, he did stay in touch with Kanye throughout the separation, and the two had summers and many holidays together. Ray West, a Christian counselor and entrepreneur, who has his own graduate degrees and was teaching college in Atlanta when Kanye was born, has lived a life expressing his creativity and accruing knowledge about the human spirit, in ways that seem to be quite parallel to his son's.

"The thing that my father definitely instilled in me—the thing I like the most—was he taught me how to think, how to use my mind," Kanye said. "A lot of parents say, 'Well, it's because I said so.' He allowed me to ask questions. I would definitely teach my son to ask as many questions as possible. Don't be afraid to be wrong. Don't be too proud to be wrong, because you can't learn anything from a compliment. Sometimes it's better to be wrong early so you can learn from it and say, 'Man, you know what? Let me see how I can change that next time.'"[1]

Ray West was one of the first African American photographers at the *Atlanta Journal-Constitution,* one of the most successful and celebrated daily newspapers in America's southeast. Ray went onto win numerous awards for photos he took for the newspaper.

Ray was also a civil rights advocate and a member of the Black Panther Party, one of the least talked about and least understood black-advocacy groups in the United States. The Black Panthers were active in the United States from the mid-1960s into the 1970s, originating on the West Coast with the goal of protecting African American neighborhoods from a growing number of police brutalities that were being tolerated by local governments. The party's goals and platforms were constantly evolving. Though it was considered socialistic in ideology, the group actually marched on California's state capitol in Sacramento to protest a ban on weapons. Members did not always agree with the ever-changing party goals, but many supported the idea of civil rights and black advocacy in the face of poverty and discrimination.

The Black Panthers created in 1968 a 10-point program that listed the following as its goals:

1. We want power to determine the destiny of our black and oppressed communities' education that teaches us our true history and our role in the present-day society.
2. We want completely free health care for all black and oppressed people.
3. We want an immediate end to police brutality and murder of black people, other people of color, all oppressed people inside the United States.
4. We want an immediate end to all wars of aggression.
5. We want full employment for our people.
6. We want an end to the robbery by the capitalists of our Black Community.
7. We want decent housing, fit for the shelter of human beings.
8. We want decent education for our people that exposes the true nature of this decadent American society.
9. We want freedom for all black and oppressed people now held in U.S. federal, state, county, city and military prisons and jails. We want trials by a jury of peers for all persons charged with so-called crimes under the laws of this country.
10. We want land, bread, housing, education, clothing, justice, peace and people's community control of modern technology.[2]

The Black Panthers lost public-image points with several demonstrations that turned violent, but many times the police were seen as harassing the Black Panthers. The leaders of the group even cried out against "black nationalism," calling it "black racism" and set goals of aligning the Black Panther Party with other parties so that it could have a more credible voice and more say in public issues and even ballot issues. However, often militant actions and constant news coverage that had the Black Panthers in conflicts with law enforcement kept the organization from many of its goals. Ray West was never one of those who associated with violence or militant behavior, he just wanted fairness—he had, after all, been among those breaking the color barrier at the Atlanta newspaper—and simply wanted to make the country more fair for his son, and himself, as well as blacks everywhere.

The only beef Ray West has with his son is use of an offensive word used to describe black people, and the profanity in Kanye's songs. Ray said he understands that Kanye had to use such words to get a foot in the door of the hip-hop listeners, but with himself established as a musician and artist, hopes Kanye will move away from that kind of language because that's not how he raised Kanye.

NOTES

1. Julie Banderas. "Interview with Donda West." *The Big Story with John Gibson,* FOX News, May 18, 2007; Jenny Eliscu. "Genius Is as Genius Does." *USA Today Weekend,* August 19, 2007.

2. Julie Banderas. "Interview with Donda West"; Aeshia Devore. "Kanye West Interview." *Teen Diaries TV,* October 9, 2007; Charles Earl Jones. *The Black Panther Party Reconsidered.* Baltimore, MD: Black Classic Press, 1998.

Chapter 3

GROWING UP IN THE HEARTLAND'S "CAPITAL" CITY

Chicago was a whole new world after Atlanta.

The unlabeled capital of the Midwest, Chicago is the hub of a critical part of America, a gateway from West to East, the Great Lakes on its doorstep. Like a lot of areas outside of the East Coast at the time, Chicago's economic relevance increased because of the railroad that opened in 1848, just nine years after the city was incorporated as Chicago. The Illinois-Michigan Canal also opened in 1848, which allowed ships from the Great Lakes to connect to the Mississippi River. This opened Chicago as a major mecca to the U.S. economic growth of the time. Chicago's growth was faster than any city in America and indeed was among the fastest in the world, going from 30,000 residents in 1850 to more than a million by 1890.

Immigrants flocked to Chicago, where among the places needing workers was the growing meatpacking industry. By 1900, Chicago had gone from a blip on the map to the fifth largest city in the world.

Chicago, however, is often noted for its spectacular strife and crises, the first of which was the Great Chicago Fire of 1871, which leveled a full third of the city, including the entire business district. From the ashes came the world's biggest (and believed first) skyscraper, the Home Insurance Building, which was the first structure of its kind to be built with structural steel. Chicago's resolve to rebuild was so strong that within 50 years of the fire, the population had tripled, to three million.

In 1893 Chicago was, in effect, opened to the eyes and mind of the world with the World's Columbian Exposition, better known as the Chicago World's Fair, in the southern suburb of Jackson Park, just north of where Kanye West's mother would buy their first home nearly 90 years later. The area before 1893 had been nothing but marshland, but the city turned it into a spectacular event that drew more than 27 million to the World's Fair, which celebrated the 400th anniversary of Columbus' "discovery" of America—a year late, though dedication ceremonies preceded it in 1892. The fair was historical and gave more history to the country, given that a young Katharine Lee Bates, an English teacher, was inspired to write "America the Beautiful." Susan B. Anthony, Thomas Edison, Annie Oakley, Frederick Douglass, and J. P. Morgan were among those at the fair.

The incredible rapid growth of the city might be credited with developing the union image that Chicago carries to this day because workers of all kinds and classes were needed to build the city into what it so quickly became. With that activity came unrest. In the 1920s, Al Capone led what came to be known as Chicago's gangster years, battling law enforcement, especially during Prohibition—when alcohol sales were banned. That did not slow growth, however, and a large number of African Americans from America's South came during that time looking for better jobs.

Chicago has ties to the infamous beginning of nuclear weapons as well; the Manhattan Project's roots were grown at the University of Chicago when a physicist conducted the first "controlled" nuclear reaction for the federal government's Manhattan Project in late 1942.

By the 1950s, the Chicago political scene was about to gain national attention, with Richard J. Daly being elected mayor, and like the rest of the country, many inner-city citizens were moving to the suburbs for better, newer, and cleaner neighborhoods with less crime.

Chicago again had the nation's, and the world's, attention with the 1968 Democratic National Convention, which came on the heels of the assassinations of likely nominee Robert F. Kennedy, younger brother of assassinated President John F. Kennedy, and civil rights leader Rev. Martin Luther King Jr., all against the backdrop of the Vietnam War. Rioting and police beatings littered the streets of Chicago. The Democratic Party was so divided that President Lyndon Johnson did not seek reelection, and the nomination went instead to Hubert Humphrey, who then lost in the election to Republican Richard Nixon. In 1989, the circle again came full, with Daley's son, Richard M. Daley, being elected Chicago's mayor.

Chicago has nearly 80 designated suburbs. The city is divided very clearly into four sections. Downtown has the "Loop," the North Side, the West Side, and the South Side, where Donda and Kanye lived.

Chicago also has a deep history in the arts, especially entertainment. The Chicago theater community originated what is known as improv, or improvisational theatre, bringing such acts as Second City, which launched the career of several *Saturday Night Live* performers. Steve Carell, star of the television show *The Office*, started in Second City, where he was understudy to his future coworker on the *Daily Show*, Stephen Colbert. Colbert went on to have his own Comedy Central program, while Carell moved on to primetime and movie superstardom.

Chapter 4

STUDIES IN THE WINDY CITY

Kanye's mother knew the importance of a solid educational foundation for her son. So when it came time to enroll him in grade school, she studied the local programs.[1] The Chicago State campus had a kindergarten, but Kanye's preschool teachers thought Kanye needed another year to mature socially, even though academically he was gifted, according to his mother's book, *Raising Kanye*. Another school was quite far away and would have been a dangerous commute in winter. Donda West found Vanderpoel Magnet School, which would be Kanye's home from kindergarten on. His mother's decision to put Kanye into one of the city's premier schools where he would get cutting-edge learning provided Kanye with a good academic environment in which he would have every chance to succeed. Kanye was enrolled in a school that had high standards for its teachers and high expectations for its students, certainly a blessing for a creative mind like Kanye's.

State universities and colleges are funded at the state level and receive federal funds as well. So although the economy might go up and down, universities are among the most stable environments and have resources such as campus libraries, gyms, and office equipment. For Donda and her young son, this stability was very important. For all the things she had to worry about in being a single mother, her job very stable. Her hours were quite manageable, and her time off could include summers if she so chose (during which she was still paid), in addition to a month at Christmas every year, plus spring break. She—and Kanye—would soon get amazing opportunities to teach abroad, something Donda took full advantage of.[2]

Though they had left a strong African American community in Atlanta, Chicago State had a high percentage of black students, so the adaptation process was not difficult for Donda—or for Kanye, in terms of any culture shock. Chicago State's history is deep; it opened in 1867 as basically a "teacher's college," but over the years it expanded into a full-service university and is fully accredited with all the standard majors and with several outstanding programs that are recognized nationally. Students can get degrees in 36 undergraduate majors and 29 graduate majors. Its 160-acre campus is on Chicago's South Side.

Kanye's mother never remarried, though she did have boyfriends with whom she and Kanye lived. These men, along with his father, whom he continued to spend time with each summer—his father eventually moved to Maryland—were, according to Donda, good role models for Kanye, leaning on him to do chores and take care of his responsibilities around the house and at school.[3] These male role models were significant for Kanye especially because he was an only child. His mother always encouraged his creativity at home and was protective of him outside the home. To that end, she stayed in close touch with his teachers.

Each of the relationships Donda had with her live-in boyfriends lasted several years, so although there was some change, life was mostly consistent for young Kanye, though he remained far closer to his mother than particularly the two men who lived with them for an extended period of time. The more significant boyfriend, who was a high school shop teacher, lived with Kanye and Donda through Kanye's adolescence and teen years and was a strict disciplinarian. Though he and Kanye clashed—and the man ultimately moved out when Kanye told his mother that he would go live with his father if the boyfriend remained—the boyfriend did have experience keeping teen boys focused and certainly added in numerous ways to Kanye's sense of responsibility.[4]

Kanye's mother said her son was designing clothes even as an elementary student. Kanye remembers deciding in fourth grade that he wanted to be a designer.[5] And while sketching out clothes and shopping with the eye of a designer even at age 10, he also was already making music. According to his mother's book, Kanye's first recorded song was a version of "Green Eggs and Ham" that he paid $25 to record at age 12 in a basement recording studio of a friend of a friend.[6]

MISSING SCHOOL, MAKING BEATS

In Chicago, Kanye still hung around at the college after school for the next few years. He used his savings and Christmas money to buy his first keyboard when he was 15 and continued writing "beats," something that he would become so prolific at that it led him to become a producer before an artist.[7]

The city of Chicago has long been a national beacon for music, from the Chicago Symphony Orchestra to both the Joffrey Ballet and Chicago Festival Ballet. The legendary band named Chicago began as the Chicago Transit Authority and still toured in 2008 after forming in the 1960s. Before Kanye, the hip-hop community of Chicago brought forth such acts as Kanye's friend and collaborator Common, Lupe Fiasco (who has recorded and toured with Kanye), Kanye's mentor No I.D., the gangsta trio Do or Die, Twista (for whom Kanye produced), Da Brat (a protégé of Jermaine Dupri), GLC, and Rhymefest, who would later co-write "Jesus Walks" with Kanye.[8]

The cultural diversification of Kanye West continued on into high school. Whereas his South Shore neighborhood was overwhelmingly black, he went to high school at Polaris in nearby Oak Lawn, another Chicago suburb, which was more than 93 percent white and just more than 1 percent black, and which in fact had more Asian American residents than African Americans. Oak Lawn, though it covers a mere 8.6 square miles, has its own musical artist royalty, with REO Speedwagon lead singer/guitarist/pianist Kevin Cronin, Irish step dancer Michael Flatley, two founding members of the band Disturbed, and the late David A. Johnston, better known as the only volcanologist killed during the Mount St. Helen's eruption in 1980 in Washington state. Johnston yelled the now famous words when the eruption started, "Vancouver, Vancouver—this is it!"

Kanye's interest in high school faded as the first two semesters kicked off. His grades took a study downward path as he focused more on music and less on homework. Formal music training for hip-hop was not embraced by local schools in most cases, so a lot of his training came from honing his own ideas and talent. He developed an ear for what sounded good and a knack for combining his beats with "samples" from songs that had been on albums, often from the likes of Michael Jackson, Luther Vandross, and other R&B acts, through the years. Wu-Tang Clan is a group Kanye often cites as a major influence, though his range of influences go from Michael Jackson to Run DMC and a host of others.

"Me and my friends talk about this all the time," Kanye said. "We think Wu-Tang had one of the biggest impacts as far as a movement, from slang to style of dress, skits, the samples."[9]

Wu-Tang remains a constant for Kanye to refer to when recounting his earliest hip-hop memories. Wu-Tang Clan was a hip-hop group of nine rappers, and that group ended up spawning Grammy winners as solo art-ists, successful producers, movie and television stars, business owners, and celebrity endorsers.

Wu-Tang was hard-core rap in every aspect and was founded by a trio of cousins. The group's name comes from the Wu Dang Mountain in central China, which is often associated with such Chinese tenets as Taoism, medicine, and martial arts, a name one of the group's founders came up with after seeing the movie Shaolin Wu Tang. The group de-veloped a significant underground following in 1993 after the release of the independent label single "Protect Ya Neck." Wu Tang did business its own way, from the start allowing all members to continue to do their own albums, which made the group hard to sign in an industry where artists gave up control of everything to record companies and manage-ment groups. In 1997 "Wu-Tang Forever" earned a Grammy nomina-tion and debuted at number 1 on Billboard. From production techniques such as a sample to how it built its image and encouraged its members to develop individually while also recording as a group, Wu-Tang became a musical phenomena, and its influence on hip-hop culture extends to this day.

CHICAGO'S HOMEGROWN HIP-HOP COMMUNITY

Kanye was a good enough student in junior high when he applied him-self, his mother told the Baltimore Sun, but later, when Kanye was in high school, she went from expecting As to hoping for Bs, and by the end of high school, she was satisfied with Kanye getting Cs because she knew he was spending all his time thinking about music during school and making beats with his friends after school, often in the bedroom of their home.[10] Kanye did go to church with his mother, and the times that they went home to Oklahoma City to visit his mother's family were filled with church and church-related events.[11]

Kanye became a part of the Chicago hip-hop movement, where he joined with a bunch of other eager rappers to form the Go-Getters, and they played in clubs throughout the city; their song "Oh, Oh, Oh" got a lot of local airtime in Chicago when Kanye was still in high school.[12]

Kanye had a few friends in high school, but only those who had a deep and real passion for music and were also interested in working on beats and writing songs after school with Kanye.

Though Jay-Z would later become a mentor and "big brother" to Kanye in New York, in Chicago it was No I.D. who got Kanye on the path to hip-hop stardom. No I.D., known as the godfather of Chicago hip-hop, made his name by honing and producing the skills of several artists, most notably Common and Jermaine Dupri. No I.D. has since worked on hit songs for Usher, Alicia Keys, and Lauryn Hill. It was Common's classic album *Resurrection* for which No I.D. remains best known. Though it only charged at number 179 on the Billboard's top 200, it was named in 1998 by *The Source* magazine as one of the top 100 rap albums of all time. So No I.D. was mentoring Kanye from the time he was 15, all the way through high school.[13]

Out of high school, Kanye was awarded a partial scholarship to study at the professional-artist school the American Academy of Arts, in downtown Chicago. The fully accredited school was founded in 1923 and offers programs in drawing and design.

Though it did not offer music, this school was clearly a perfect fit at least for Kanye's interests in interior design and fashion design and his deft drawing skills. However, soon after starting, Kanye grew tired of creating what others wanted him to create, whether it was a specific sort of format or object. He already had in his mind what he wanted to do, which was write, make, and produce hip-hop music. Still, the time at the Academy of Art certainly had an effect on him and developed further some of his artistic skills and interpretative artistic understandings. Ironically, Kanye, the self-proclaimed dropout, was probably not a good fit for classes based in theory. Yet everything done well is grounded in fundamentally sound theory, whether it is art design mixing and matching colors and patterns or rhyming lyrics by sometimes using words that actually do not rhyme. The person doing it might not realize it, but if it is being done well, it is based on good theoretical background. At the Academy of Arts, when he chose to attend class, he picked up bits and pieces of what goes through an artist's mind—and what should be kept in mind—in creating art. By having to answer the occasional question from a teacher and through getting feedback on a project, Kanye was picking up pieces of information that would expand his artistic horizons. The experience at the Academy of Arts told Kanye West that he did not want to be designing brochures for other people or doing commissioned artistic work that required him to work from other people's specifications.

When he dropped out of art school, his mother desperately wanted him to continue in college. Her own commitment to education was exceeded by no one in her own family or anyone she had gone to school with—she had, after all, reached the highest echelons of education with the most advanced academic degree offered. She had already been around thousands of students herself when she was in school getting her degrees, and she had taught thousands of students as a college professor, and she saw what happened to students who dropped out—they rarely ever returned, especially later in life as family and work became a priority.

So Donda went to work finding another college option for him. Kanye was pretty much out of options.[14] The only option remaining was Chicago State University. Donda also realized her son needed to have an eye kept on him, so what better, she decided, than to have him be an English major at Chicago State University. She could help him with his schoolwork, stay on top of him by staying in touch with her colleagues to see how he was doing in class, and give him the push he clearly needed to recognize his academic potential. Whether he actually used the degree itself would be another matter, one that was not that important to Donda West at the time; as she said in countless interviews and her own book, she had been taught, and had seen firsthand, that young people needed a college degree to start out with a chance in their adult life.

At Chicago State, Kanye had to start over, forced to take freshman composition, which teaches the basics of good writing but usually with specific assigned topics or at least those assigned by the teacher. Though attendance was a problem, Kanye went to enough classes to hear what good writing is and is not.[15] He had good grounding in the fundamentals of the language—whether he wanted to break them or adhere to them— and of what constitutes good writing.

His teachers, according to Donde West's book, told his mother that Kanye did not want to be in their classes, and that rather than be in class, he was often in the music department at the college. So he was, she said, thinking of beats, rhyme, and verse while teachers were talking about opening paragraphs, persuasive rhetoric, and transitions, but some schooling on the formalities of English usage was certainly better for his musical ambitions than working at a fast-food restaurant would have been.[16] He had to turn in assignments, and whether he agreed with what he was assigned and was told to do or not, by having to read textbooks about English and other subjects, and at least occasionally sit through lectures, he picked up some basics and fundamentals that would serve him well. The college also had music rooms that he frequented, so as had been the case since his mother moved him from Atlanta more than 15 years earlier, Kanye's time on the college campus was still stimulating him and helping him grow as a learner and an artist.

Kanye's time at Chicago State came to an end in 1998; he was not going to class all the time, his teachers reported, according to West's book. One of his teachers said that although she liked Kanye as a person, she would prefer not to have him in class, a sentiment Kanye himself shared; that is, he had no desire to be in school, either. That was it. Game over.

Kanye West was done with college, or college was done with Kanye West. Either way, he had his freedom from school, but his mother told him he would pay rent and get a job—by age 20 though, Kanye had a different kind of a degree, one that said "co-producer" for tracks by hip-hop artists Harlem World and Mad Rapper.

MUSICAL PATH

Chicago State was not without its notable alums in the music industry. Although Chicago State was an urban school set in the south suburbs of the central United States, one of the most influential bands of the 1980s were Chicago State alum: Dennis DeYoung and several other founding members of the rock band Styx (Tommy Shaw was not from Chicago State). It was, however, Dennis DeYoung who crafted Styx's most memorable songs, including "Babe," "The Best of Times," and "Lady." He was largely known as the voice of Styx through the band's heyday atop the charts, and the band was considered one of the few legitimate stadium acts of its time. DeYoung has a music degree from Chicago State—it is interesting to ponder whether Kanye would have stayed and seen through his degree at the university had he been in the music department, given that his time spent at Chicago State was often in the music rooms, not in the English building during his assigned class times.

DeYoung is most widely known, aside from the songs he wrote to put Styx in the "super group" category, for what can best be called his artistically technological foray in "Mr. Roboto," which featured a futuristic beat and melody that was, at the time, revolutionary and years ahead of its time in the music scene. The song and others on the album—titled *Kilroy Was Here*—along with the synthesizer work, were an immediate hit with fans. However, like Kanye, DeYoung had interests working more outside of the proverbial box than doing what was standard.

Unlike Kanye, DeYoung's passion for artistic exploration ended his, and the band's, appeal to stadium audiences. DeYoung created, directed, and produced a stage show with "Mr. Roboto" as its focus, the choppy, robot-like movements and lights and sound all part of the gig. Artistically and on a theater stage, it might well have been seen as genius. In front of hyped rock fans who wanted to either bang their heads or at the very least sing along, it proved to be torture. The band ultimately split over that, and other, artistic differences, and the band that brought "Too Much Time on My Hands" and "Come Sail Away" to audiences around the world had few options and plenty of time on its hands as its career faded off into the distance. Yet DeYoung came back and played the role of

Jesus in the touring stage show of *Jesus Christ, Superstar* in the early 1990s. He was truly ahead of his time, though out of touch with his audience, at, as it turned out, the most significant moment, as other bands in the early 1980s were waiting to pounce on audience share and gathering a good fan base, something Styx enjoyed throughout the 1970s and early 1980s. "Mr. Roboto" was the end of Styx for Tommy Shaw, who left the group to play his own more rock-oriented music in 1984. Styx faded shortly thereafter, and a re-configured Styx, with Tommy Shaw but not DeYoung, tours separately these days, with the nostalgia of the 1970s and 1980s music and for 50-something-year-old fans. DeYoung also continues as a solo performer, doing his Styx-era songs, and in 2007, he returned to his rock roots with a new album that made it to the top of the Canadian charts.

NOTES

1. Donda Clairann Williams West. Dissertation abstract. Auburn University, 1980.

2. Donda West. *Raising Kanye: Life Lessons from the Mother of a Hip-Hop Superstar.* New York: Pocket Books, 2007.

3. Ibid.

4. Greg Kot. "Rapper's Rise: From South Side to Top of the Charts." *Chicago Tribune,* February 11, 2004, http://www.rocafella.com/News.aspx?item=101084&sectionid=137.

5. Katy O'Donnell. "Kanye West's Mother on Parenting and More." *Baltimore Sun* blogs, September 2007, http://weblogs.baltimoresun.com/entertainment/critics/blog/2007/09/kanye_wests_mother_on_parentin.html.

6. Donda West. *Raising Kanye.*

7. Ibid.

8. Kimberly Davis. "Kanye West: Hip-Hop's New Big Shot." *Ebony,* April 2005.

9. George Lang. "Rap Star's Mom Left a Legacy." *The Oklahoman,* November 20, 2007.

10. Kimberly Davis. "Kanye West."

11. Greg Kot. "Rapper's Rise."

12. Donda West. *Raising Kanye.*

13. Greg Kot. "Rapper's Rise."

14. Luke Bainbridge. "It's Kanye's World." *(London) Observer,* August 12, 2007.

15. Donda West. *Raising Kanye.*

16. Ibid.

Chapter 5

HELLO, HIP-HOP

While all this was going on in the smaller world of Kanye West, as a movement, hip-hop was snowballing.

Though hip-hop is a relatively new genre as a major player in the music industry, it has actually been around for nearly 50 years. Hip-hop is believed to have had its start in the Bronx, a borough of New York City.

A lot of listeners think that rap and hip-hop are the same thing, but this is not necessarily the case. Rap is the act alone of rapping, and hip-hop includes the rap with a beat. Another term for rapping is emceeing, which spawned the term MC, which is the act of rapping with rhythm and rhyme. The "beat" or music usually is "sampled," which means taken from another song.

The music's roots are from West Africa and African Americans, and the disc jockeys at the New York City neighborhood parties would isolate the percussion breaks from popular songs, the most recognizable parts and the part that was danced to, something that Jamaicans—who were a big part of several Bronx neighborhoods, including one of the pioneers of hip-hop, DJ Kool Herc—are believed to have brought to hip-hop music. The heavy emphasis on drum and bass, or "dub," is from American sailors playing music in Jamaica, who took the music and used the drum and bass and came up with their own rap to go along with it. This spread to New York City as a considerable number of Jamaicans immigrated, especially to the Bronx, and hip-hop became a significant part of New York City culture.

Many of the most famous raps include music from songs popular long ago, from rhythm and blues music to soul and even pop music. A sample can come from a previous record, or it can be a DJ, or disc jockey, who uses records spun both forward and backward, drum machines, and synthesizers. Live bands, including horn sections—used particularly well in Kanye's "Touch the Sky"—are becoming more prevalent in modern rap.

When hip-hop started getting popular with the general public in the late 1970s, an MC would often introduce a DJ and the music to get the audience interested. So the MC was literally an emcee in the traditional sense, keeping the audience excited and into the show, telling jokes and stories, which evolved into the MC rapping. Soon enough the rapping and music overlapped, and the genre of hip-hop had a unique style, involving much more music to the poetic rap. Turntables were used, playing the music forward and backward, the scratchy sound becoming a trademark of the genre.[1]

The looping, remixing, and sampling from older records became an art form, along with the raps that were done to the music. Break-dancing also became part of the festivities at hip-hop block parties. The music's beat and the bass were significant hallmarks of the music, and many people who have neighbors who listen loudly to hip-hop, or cars that go by with it playing loudly, can usually hear or even be literally shaken by the beat and powerful bass line, even if they can't hear the lyrics. Grandmaster Flash and the Furious Five's Keith Cowboy are credited with creating the term "hip-hop," with the story being that Cowboy's friend had joined the army and, mocking the "left, right, left, right" marching, instead, said "Hip, hop, hip, hop." Furious Five rapper Melle Mel is largely believed to be the first to call himself an MC. Hip-hop artist Kurtis Blow did a soft drink commercial, becoming the first of the genre to get a mainstream endorsement deal, but he was just as quickly labeled by hip-hop fans and other artists as a sellout.

Though many notable MCs and DJs came before him, LL Cool J became the most well-known hip-hop artist in the 1980s. Throughout the decade, hip-hop spread. In the early 1990s, "gangsta rap" began to take over the scene, thanks to a lot of well-publicized controversy. Ice-T's song "Cop Killer," which was originally done by a hard rock band to much less fanfare, became big as rap hit big-time in the 1990s. Police brutality was in the news, particularly in Los Angeles, and Ice-T's song was portrayed by the media and some politicians as promoting violence toward police. Rap and hip-hop did not try to shake their connection to violence. Many rappers were from the various boroughs of New York City, from violent housing projects where gangs, drugs, and guns were a part of daily life. Several conservative congressmen, along with the wife of eventual Democratic Vice President Al Gore, pushed for Congressional hearings to draw attention to the violent and sexually promiscuous lyrics of rap and hip-hop albums, leading several stores to either not carry the albums or include on the cover a warning about the profane, violent, and sexual lyrics.

Public Enemy became a rap force with its 1987 album *Yo, Bum Rush the Show* on Def Jam. Kanye said his father's message of activism coincided with Public Enemy's music. Kanye said the only reason his father, Ray West, would put up with Kanye playing Public Enemy is because he had heard the message Public Enemy was trying to get out through its music.

Along with Kurtis Blow and LL Cool J, other notable artists to emerge included Run-DMC, which did what is now considered a breakthrough and classic rap with Aerosmith to "Walk This Way." The Beastie Boys came out with "You've Got to Fight (for Your Right to Party)" and became a force in the genre for decades to come.

Gangsta rap went full throttle with NWA, which as a group would sell more than nine million albums in the 1980s and early 1990s, even though most of their songs were banned from many U.S. radio stations because most of the tracks were about sex, drugs, and violence—this was before music could be downloaded, and before the Internet was available to the public. NWA came out of Compton, California, widely regarded as one of the most gang-infested areas in the country. In fact, Ice-T did the theme song to the movie *Colors*, referring to the red of the Bloods gang and the blue of the Crips gang. So intense was the rivalry that young men would be shot if seen wearing blue in a Bloods neighborhood or red in a Crips-controlled area. NWA's debut not only made the West Coast hip-hop artists a player in the industry, but also ignited the East Coast–West Coast battle that would, at times, be lethal. NWA's members included Dr. Dre, Ice Cube, Eazy-E, and MC Ren, all of whom went on to be successful solo artists, and Dr. Dre in particular became one of the most accomplished music producers and label executives of all time. Many of NWA's songs were protests against police brutality and profiling and even drew a letter of response from the FBI, which urged the label not to promote violence or attacks on police. The letter only served to bolster the group as gangsta rappers and to build its following. After NWA split up, the members took digs at each other in their rap lyrics.

Dr. Dre, of the West Coast scene, took gangsta to a new level with his 1992 album *The Chronic*, which introduced the G Funk style, using lowered tempos with funk music.

NO MORE SCHOOL: IT'S A (W)RAP

Though hip-hop was turning into an economic locomotive, Kanye West was not about to leave Chicago State without a degree—if his mother had her way.[2] Donda knew as well as anyone that simply having a college degree carried with it respect and honor in the real world. "It was drummed into my head that college is the ticket to a good life," Donda West said. "But some career goals don't require college. For Kanye to make an album called 'College Dropout,' it was more about having the guts to embrace who you are, rather than following the path society has carved out for you. And that's what Kanye did."[3]

Meanwhile, after dropping out of college for the second time in two years, Kanye West had time on his hands, and his mother knew that would not fly. Regardless, he kept on with the music. Local hip-hop producer/ artist No I.D. introduced him to another outstanding producer and artist, Jermaine Dupri, who utilized Kanye's talent and beat for the song "Turn It Out" on Dupri's album *Life in 1472*.[4]

As a result of this collaboration, Kanye's name was getting bigger with the movers in the rap industry. Through his association with No I.D., and having sold a beat to a song that was produced, Kanye got a meeting at Columbia in New York with, as it turned out, Michael Mauldin, who was Jermaine Dupri's father.[5] When Kanye claimed, according to press reports, that he would be bigger than Michael Jackson and better than Jermaine Dupri, Kanye claimed to not know Mauldin was Dupri's father.[6] Regardless, the reference did not inspire faith from Mauldin, who sent Kanye back to Chicago without a record deal and with no hopes for another. During this time Kanye had moved out of his mother's house, after dropping out of school and realizing that the meeting with Mauldin and Columbia, though not germinating into anything he could harvest, was a sign that he could compete at that level. So he was off. The question was, where? He first settled on Atlanta.

He got an apartment, put down a deposit, and then thought about it: All the best rap was coming out of New York. New York was, after all, where the movement was, where the action was, and it was where the labels were that were creating the likes of Jay-Z and other stars.[7]

No I.D. also introduced Kanye to Kyambo Joshua, aka "Hip-Hop Joshua," who was the director of Artists and Repertoire, better known as A&R, which means finding and developing new talent, for Roc-A-Fella's label, and Joshua signed Kanye to produce records for the label. No I.D. has released three of his own works since 1997 and, after producing a pair of songs for Jay-Z's *American Gangster* in 2007, began working on tracks for Nas and Rhymefest.[8]

After the aborted move to Atlanta,[9] Kanye decided to go to New York—though he lived more affordably nearby in Newark, New Jersey at first—after selling some of his own music for several thousand dollars to Jermaine Dupri.[10]

Although it was not a ton of money, certainly not enough to get rich off of, it did get him on his way and into a New Jersey apartment.[11] It was, in other words, a dangerous amount because it gave him enough money to place a bet, on himself, one that he had spent the past years clamoring for, so sure he was of himself that he just needed the backing—success, he was positive, was the only thing that could possibly follow once he had the opportunity.

He moved to New York. One thing quickly led to another, and there he was, in the studio, producing songs for the likes of Alicia Keyes and, of course, the man who would shape him professionally like no one else, Jay-Z.[12]

Though Kanye was an immediate success as a producer, he realized he would have a hard time selling himself as an artist to the powers-that-be at hip-hop labels.

"It was a strike against me that I didn't wear baggy jeans and jerseys and that I never hustled, never sold drugs," West said. "But for me to have the opportunity to stand in front of a bunch of executives and present myself, I had to hustle in my own way. I can't tell you how frustrating it was that they didn't get that. No joke, I'd leave meetings crying all the time.[13]

THE UN-DROPOUT: DONDA WEST

Kanye West's mother, with her many academic achievements, could be viewed as having the academic sort of superstar status that her son achieved in the music business.

She grew up in Oklahoma City, went to Virginia Union for her undergraduate, and attended Atlanta University for her master's degree in English. As a scholar, she had reached the highest levels as a professor, earned a doctorate, and worked as department chair of Chicago State University in a major U.S. city, arguably the third most high-profile behind New York and Los Angeles.

Kanye West's mother started an amazingly long route to get what is called her "terminal degree," which in higher education can be a master's of fine arts, but is more often a doctorate, or PhD. Though both are terminal degrees, only the PhD carries the title of doctor, which many colleges consider more prestigious. In fact, outside of English and theater, most faculty members at four-year universities and colleges are required to get a PhD.

When Donda West finished her undergraduate degree, or bachelor's, she moved on to do a master's degree. After two long years of graduate school, Donda West had her master's degree, joining the community of scholars with advanced degrees.

But this scholar was not done. A few years before Kanye's birth, Donda committed more than three more years to her life to study at Auburn University in Alabama to get her PhD. But Donda, as she always was when it came to schoolwork, was up to the challenge. She stayed focused and made it through the coursework at Auburn, which is no small feat in itself.[14]

Donda was shaped as a mother by understanding how to teach children, studying pedagogy—the art of how to effectively teach—in graduate school. So although she was not one to sing her own virtues as a single parent, she already had the classroom experience of knowing how children learned, how to recognize special needs or creative abilities, and how to manage young men and women.[15] As the abstract from her dissertation indicates, Donda was studying language, something her son would make a career out of.

KANYE AND DONDA: LANGUAGE IS "SITUATIONAL"

Donda West pointed out in several interviews that language that might seem inappropriate in some circles—for example, in hip-hop lyrics—could be completely appropriate in others. This is called "situational" language. Some do not like the slang used in rap music, including some of Kanye's lyrics, and Donda West does not defend words that she also finds offensive, but she does defend the use of those words for artistic purposes. For example, if a husband put on some weight, and his wife came into the kitchen and called him fat, the man might laugh or smile. If a stranger on the street walked past him and said, "Look out, Chubby," it could result in a fist fight. In one situation, the word is playful, perhaps even a term of endearment and affection. In another situation, the word is offensive and lacks even the most basic tact.

Donda defined as situational words and phrases that might be properly used in one moment, or even one sentence, but that possibly have a very different meaning in another setting, or even sentence. And only the critical thinker or the person saying the words can really understand the intended message. This is something Kanye also explained.

"People who write stuff paraphrase," West said. "They take what I'm saying—and I speak in colors—and flip it to black and white. Sometimes, I might say something that has four or five meanings. If I'm being sarcas-

tic, they'll take out the set-up or the punch line and I sound like a jerk.
It's the edit."[16]

Before it became a part of Donda's scholarship and her son's artistic
repertoire, situational language was a big movement from the 1930s to
1960s by linguistic scholars in Great Britain. Given that it was founded by
linguists, it is obviously based on oral communication. The same could be
said for hip-hop lyrics, which are often personal or even autobiographical
lines as an artist tells a story to the listeners. The words in a rap song are
not always lyrical prose befitting of a best-selling novel, but they quickly
and concisely get a particular message across to listeners. The British situational language scholars noted four key points that apply to hip-hop di-
rectly. First of all, language learning is habit-forming. If children are raised
using certain words a certain way, that will be ingrained in their minds, for
both hearing it and using it. Second, language skills are better taught and
better learned if they are first presented orally, or spoken. This is an important factor for teaching language, even English. Hearing a word, and
seeing facial expressions and inflection of tone, can affect how the word
is used, whether it is something that sounds especially unique or causes
eyebrows to raise. It is tested out orally and then applied on paper.

Third, the meanings of words can only be learned in cultural context.
This connects to the first point, but it is even more an attempt to point
out that people from varying backgrounds and diverse cultures learn and
experience language different. What is more unique than seeing on a television show how an offensive word in America is just slang for a household
object in England? Words have different meanings to different people.
Fourth, the British linguists noted how the better foundation for learning
was analogy rather than analysis. Analogy is a big part of rap songs—an
analogy is similarities between the like features of two words, which allow
comparisons to be made. That is something key in hip-hop lyrics. There
is a fifth point made by the scholars, and though it does not apply as
uniformly as the other four, it is worth considering: Mistakes need to be
avoided because they make bad habits. Yes, and no. On the one hand,
Donda and other English scholars certainly wanted to teach their students
the correct way to write sentences, structure papers, and use grammar. We
all remember subject, verb, and predicate from sentence diagramming.
However, if one knows the rules well, those rules can be broken at times.
The sentence earlier—"Yes, and no"—breaks every rule of subject, verb,
and predicate, yet the reader gets the point that it is saying the previous
sentence is both true and false. Rules are good, and as a society we live by
them, but when writing, a talented author or hip-hop artist can do things
that aren't "by the rules" and make them work. One of Kanye's biggest

breakthroughs in hip-hop music cited by critics is the way he uses words that do not rhyme yet makes them sound alike by emphasizing a syllable, or saying the words in a way that portends a rhyme without changing its meaning. This gets the message from the artist to the listener even though it breaks a rule by not rhyming.

"I take stuff that I know appeals to people's bad sides and match it up with stuff that appeals to their good side," West told *Time* magazine in August 2005.

Kanye also samples, extensively, and uses songs from long ago, the 1960s and 1970s, that would not seem to connect in any possible way, shape, or form to what he is rapping about on his songs. But this is a kind of situational use of music. The beats West uses are woven seamlessly with his drum machine and other instruments, and the songs flow. Often, the lyrics from the previous song are loosely connected to his song, such as the song "Diamonds from Sierra Leone," in which Kanye sampled from a James Bond theme done by Shirley Bassey in 1971. The connection that Kanye makes between "diamonds are forever," the title of the James Bond movie, and the killings in Sierra Leone over diamonds—a kind of forever in terms of eternity—is something that adds a "thinking" element to most of Kanye's songs.

Certainly, sampling and "hooks" are nothing new to hip-hop music, but the thought that goes into each one by West seems to generate as much critical thinking as it does musical entertainment, something his mother, as a scholar, was certainly very proud of.

With her doctorate complete, Donda West pursued a tenure-track college professor job. This is the lifestyle Donda West raised Kanye in when they moved to Chicago when Kanye was 3 years old. Many would consider the intellectually stimulating and comparatively safe college setting a safe and more stable situation for a single mother raising a young child than most other options. Donda had worked and studied hard to put herself in a position for a well-respected, stable, and decent-paying career with good benefits that provided job security and continued her own intellectual growth.[17] This was a career where she would help young people better their language skills and prepare them for the real world, even help them get on track to chase their dreams. One of those she helped most was Kanye.

NOTES

1. Terry Moran. "Home with Kanye West." *Nightline*, ABC News, September 24, 2007.

2. Ibid.

3. Donda West. *Raising Kanye: Life Lessons from the Mother of a Hip-Hop Superstar*. New York: Pocket Books, 2007.

4. Jody Rosen. "Way Out West." *Blender*, October 2007.

5. Greg Kot. "Rapper's Rise: From South Side to Top of the Charts." *Chicago Tribune*, February 11, 2004, http://www.rocafella.com/News.aspx?item=101084&sectionid=137.

6. Austin Skaggs. "Troublemaker of the Year." *Rolling Stone*, December 15, 2005.

7. Shaheem Reid. "Kanye, Run-DMC, Outkast, Justin Sound Off on Our Top 10 Hip-Hop Groups." MTV.com, March 6, 2007.

8. Donda West. *Raising Kanye*.

9. Ibid.

10. George Lang. "Rap Star's Mom Left a Legacy." *The Oklahoman*, November 20, 2007.

11. Donda West. *Raising Kanye*.

12. Simon Vozick-Levinson. "Jay-Z's Brotherly Love." Music Q&A. *Entertainment Weekly Online*, Fall 2007.

13. Josh Tyrangiel. "Why You Can't Ignore Kanye." *Time*, August 21, 2005.

14. Donda West. *Raising Kanye*.

15. George Lang. "Rap Star's Mom Left a Legacy."

16. Nui Te Koha. "Kanye's New Sort of Rap." *(Australia) Sunday Mail*, September 16, 2007.

17. Julie Banderas. Interview with Donda West. *The Big Story with John Gibson*, FOX News, May 18, 2007.

Chapter 6

THE LOUIS VUITTON DON

Kanye ties fashion into music, noting that good taste extends across the boundaries of one's interests. On British television Kanye said that people who are really into fashion listen to Franz Ferdinand, George Michael, and even Boy George's Culture Club tracks, yet the only hip-hop songs they have are from Jay-Z and Kanye himself.

In an interview broadcast on *Teen Diaries*, West displayed much pride in the fact that a major magazine had tabbed him one of the best dressers in the world. "I went to art school, so I'm getting heavy into design—you know, shoes and clothes," West said. "I'd go to Polo, Louis Vuitton, Marc Jacobs, or whatever and say to myself, 'Man, if they dial the color like this, I would like it better.' I'm just looking for opportunities to really apply my art to stuff I love."[1]

From the beginning Kanye never thought it would be acceptable to let someone design a line of clothes with his name on it and just stamp his name on the collar. Rather, he would be not just involved, but running the show, from start to finish.

"A lot of celebrities walk in, and there will be designers who have worked on stuff their entire lives, and the [designer] says, 'Hey, you take this, this is what I picture for you,'" West said, noting he started designing his own stuff "because people couldn't do exactly what it is I wanted to do. Just like with producing and making my own videos and stuff like, that, I had to learn how to do it so I could present to the world something new and different. I want something that's really respected. I wanted to be a designer before I wanted to be a rapper. Rapping has given me a plateau to meet with some really dope designers. It's taken years, but I'm learning a lot."[2]

As Kanye West's career took off, West talked often about building the "Kanye West brand." He compared himself to Disney, Coca-Cola, and McDonald's, saying that when people got something with Kanye West on it, they knew the quality was second to none. They not only knew what they were getting every time, but knew that it would be good too.[3]

Branding has been very popular and important to businesses through the years. As entertainers have become wealthy the last 20 or so years, more have focused on building their name as a brand and diversifying themselves outside of the area in which they gained fame, which in Kanye's case of course would be hip-hop music. That's not to say they distance themselves from their bread and butter. Rather, they use what they have done in one area to give them leverage in another area and to build reputable products in other areas, through endorsements and even original lines of clothing, such as Jay-Z has done, and healthy drinks, as 50 Cent did with his vitamin water, and other areas that are tied more closely to their music fame, such as video games.[4]

Corporations have done this for more than a century. Nike is more tied to sports, but it started out as shoes before branching into apparel, swimsuits, footballs, workout gloves, golf equipment, and equipment for most other sports. Michael Jordan became a brand at the top of his game. In addition to endorsing the widest range of products ever for an athlete, ranging from sports drinks and shoes to underwear and cologne, the Jordan brand was built on Jordan's basketball success. Quality, however, is very important. Wayne Gretzky, widely regarded as the greatest hockey player ever—and who built his own brand by moving NHL teams from Canadian outpost Edmonton to Los Angeles toward the end of his career—put his name on a hand-operated hockey game that did not work properly. Fans took it as a slight by Gretzky himself, even though he was only a paid endorser, and the Gretzky brand suffered a big setback from the negative publicity generated by the faulty game.

Kanye West has never been interested in just one area of the arts. As mentioned, he was designing clothes as a fourth grader. What West is now trying to do by designing for Louis Vuitton is to stretch himself artistically and as an entertainer. He wants to create something called "salience," creating awareness of the Kanye West brand and appreciation for its attributes, such as a commitment to quality, but in Kanye's case also a commitment to looking good and being trend-setting.[5] A brand has to have benefits that resonate with consumers, that a buying public would consider important.

Louis Vuitton is a high-end, high-quality brand. The French company is known for its fashion and leather goods. When it signed Kanye West in 2008, Kanye joined such Louis Vuitton staples as fashion designer Marc Jacobs, who makes some of the priciest, most sought-after—and most illegally counterfeited—fashion bags in the world. Model Gisele Bundchen is also a Louis Vuitton collaborator. Louis Vuitton resides in the rarified fashion air that includes Prada, Versace, Gucci, and Chanel.

People hoping to see a picture of Louis Vuitton himself when the deal with Kanye West was announced were more than a century late; Vuitton started the company in Paris, France, in 1854, making high-quality trunks for storage and transporting items. Vuitton introduced lightweight, airtight trunks that were flat-bottomed and made of trianon canvas. Before Vuitton, trunks were rounded, which was great for helping water runoff and not ruining the trunks, but the rounding made the trunks impossible for stacking. The flat trunk was perfect for stacking, particularly for travel, which wealthy people did frequently, and of course they needed trunk upon trunk to take their things. After starting in Paris, Louis Vuitton opened a store in London, England, in 1885. He died seven years later, in 1892, and his son, Georges Vuitton, took over the business.

The trunk was functional and fashionable, and Georges Vuitton took the design and used it on leather bags, purses, and wallets. This built the brand and created brand equity. Audrey Hepburn, in fact, in the movie *Charade* has a Louis Vuitton bag. Georges opened stores in Japan in 1978. In 1987 Louis Vuitton got together with high-end champagne manufacturer Moet et Chandon and brandy maker Hennessy to form a luxury goods conglomerate. Taking the first letters from Moet and Hennessy, the LVMH brand had its profits increase nearly 50 percent in one year. The company came out with a pen collection and in 1998 made Marc Jacobs its fashion designer. Stores continued to open around the world, including in Beijing, China, and Morocco. Jacobs created a graffiti-over-monogram pattern line of Vuitton bags that became must-haves for high societies, especially celebrities. Bracelets and watches from LVHS followed. For Louis Vuitton's 150th anniversary in 2004, it opened a Fifth Avenue store in New York City. Though luggage remains a staple, its use of celebrities and well-known public figures for its goods has built its brand into an industry leader in all areas it produces.

One of those brand-building events was hosting Kanye West's 30th birthday party in 2007, attended by hip-hop artists, models, and other celebrities. In July 2008, Kanye and Louis Vuitton announced that Kanye would design men's shoes for the company. Kanye also told media at the annual Paris fashion extravaganza that he was working on developing a women's wear collection, though he did not say for which company he would design women's wear.

Kanye has also written a fashion column off and on, for *Complex*, an entertainment magazine. At Louis Vuitton's 2008 Paris show debuting the 2009 LV line, Kanye said that he grew up with the Louis Vuitton look and that he has always admired the company's style.[6]

DIDDY'S FASHION FORAY WAS FIRST

But before there was Kanye, there was Diddy, aka Sean Combs, Puff Daddy, P. Diddy, Puffy, and now, just plain Diddy. Kanye refers to Diddy as one of the pioneers of rap artists going into multiple genres and products, particularly fashion and pop culture, to promote themselves and their music. Unlike Kanye, Diddy does have the "street cred" that most of the New York City–area rappers are proud to boast about. In fact, Diddy was raised in Harlem's public housing project and grew up in the Bronx. When he was just three years old, his father was shot in his car after leaving a party. Several gangsters in New York publicly admitted being tied to Diddy's father in the early 1970s. Diddy was a high school football standout, and one of his teammates went on to become a known associate of the Gambino crime family.

After graduating high school in 1987, Diddy attended the well-respected black college Howard University, where he made a name for himself first not as an artist, but as a promoter and marketer for events, which eventually led to an internship at Uptown Records. After commuting back and forth from school in Washington, D.C., to New York to work at Uptown, he quit college because Uptown hired him full-time, where he developed talent and even was the one to sign Mary J. Blige. His first rap event brought his first court case, as a Heavy D concert at a New York college event center ended in a near riot, causing a stampede in which nine people were killed.

But that Heavy D event showed Diddy his future could be in rap, and the year following the concert, he signed with a Connecticut DJ to start a label dedicated to developing rap artists. Though the two split before it became reality, Diddy stayed employed by Uptown until 1993, when he was fired, but he left with something of great value—the rap artist Notorious B.I.G., around whom Diddy built his new venture, Bad Boy Records. Diddy signed and produced hugely successful acts, including Faith Evans, Usher, Mariah Carey, Boyz II Men, and a host of hip-hop artists led by the Notorious B.I.G.

The rappers on the West Coast took notice, and Suge Knight and Tupac took turns taking potshots at Diddy and Notorious B.I.G., sending the West Coast–East Coast feud to an explosive level.

Finally, in 1997, Diddy, then known as Puff Daddy, was, like Kanye West would later be, so accomplished as a producer that he needed to do his own work. Diddy's debut "Can't Nobody Hold Me Down," was Billboard's number 1 hit for six weeks, and the album from which it came, *No Way Out*, won the Best Rap Grammy in 1998.

Diddy crossed genres and had a smash hit, "Come with Me," with rock legend Jimmy Page for the movie *Godzilla*. In the late 1990s, critics took aim at Diddy for his extensive use of other artists' songs, known as sampling, in his own work. And in 1999, Diddy's world turned violent. A studio session was interrupted by gunfire. And then his girlfriend at the time, JLo, aka Jennifer Lopez, a successful singer and actress, was with him when gunfire broke out at a Manhattan nightclub. Diddy was indicted on weapons charges, though O.J. Simpson lawyer Johnny Cochran got Diddy acquitted.

Appearing in movies such as *Made* and *Monster's Ball*, Diddy received critical praise but was in constant scraps with the law. From there Diddy worked with such pop artists as Britney Spears and 'N Sync, collaborated with rock icon David Bowie, and signed the pop girl group Dream to his label. Diddy opened in 2002 for 'N Sync on tour.

But he also ran the 2003 New York City Marathon and raised $2 million for school children in New York City and headed a voter-registration campaign in 2004.

Diddy brought the concept of Renaissance man to the hip-hop world before Kanye West did. By building his brand outside of music, Diddy has been estimated to be worth between $340 and $350 million, making him, along with Jay-Z, probably one of the richest hip-hop artists ever, though others are well above the $100 million mark as well, including 50 Cent, Jay-Z, and Dr. Dre.

Diddy owns Bad Boy records and, like Kanye, has an interest in clothes. But Diddy has already brought his clothing line, Sean John (John is his legal middle name), to market, leaving him a few steps ahead of Kanye. In 2004 Diddy's clothing line won the Menswear Designer of the Year award from the Council of Fashion Designers of America. His company suffered a public relations nightmare when it was discovered the clothes were made under sweatshop-like conditions in the Central American nation of Honduras. However, Diddy stepped in, had a union formed for employees, and put in air conditioning and a water-purification system, making the plant a flagship for both NAFTA-inspired business and what a celebrity can use their clout for, to help workers.

Diddy has also become a multimedia entrepreneur, producing and starring in the reality show *Making the Band* and appearing on Broadway.

Though Diddy sold his label to Warner in 2005, he still released a 2006 album, his first since 2002, on Bad Boy Records, and with an all-star guest list ranging from Outkast to Christina Aguilera, it debuted at number 1 on the charts. In August 2008, *I Want to Work for Diddy*, another reality show, debuted on the MTV-owned VH1.

Outkast is another band, even though it is composed of members not even a generation ahead of Kanye, that influenced him. Kanye said that he and Outkast share similarities, including trying to do something new and different with their music and making music not for radio stations but for listeners. Kanye also said that Outkast is stylish, something on which he too prides himself.

Like Diddy, Kanye's interest in design in not just for fashion purposes—though that is the area in which Kanye is likely to make his biggest design impression.

NOTES

1. Aeshia Devore. "Kanye West Interview." *Teen Diaries TV*, October 9, 2007. Retrieved from YouTube via http://www.TeenDiariesOnline.com.

2. *Popworld*. "Kanye West Interview." Channel 4, Great Britain, July 8, 2007.

3. Aeshia Devore. "Kanye West Interview."

4. Kenneth Clow and Donald Blaack. *Integrated Advertising Promotion, and Marketing Communications*. Upper Saddle River, NJ: Pearson-Prentice Hall, 2007.

5. Amy Spencer. "A Fashionable Life." *Harper's Bazaar*, August 2007, http://www.harpersbazaar.com/fashion/fashion-articles/fashionable-life-west-0807.

6. Edie Cohen. "Hip-Hop and Pop." *Interior Design*, August 2007, http://www.interiordesign.net/id_article/CA6469699/id.

Chapter 7

DR. DRE PAVED PATH FROM (THE) WEST

Dr. Dre became a well-known artist as part of the hard-core rap group NWA, which gained fame and infamy with violent lyrics describing the hard-core street life in his hometown of gang-infested Compton, California. It is not as well known that Dre, whose real name is Andre Romelle Young, started out as a club DJ who went by "Dr. J," after the famous basketball star Julius Irving. In 1986 Dre hooked up with Ice T and recorded songs for Ruthless Records, owned by admitted drug dealer and rapper Eazy-E.

But Dr. Dre became a major player in the industry finally in 1992, when the infamous Death Row Records sprung to life. Dre was able to get out of NWA after his bodyguard Suge Knight persuaded the powers that be to release Dre from his commitments to the group. Dr. Dre collaborated with Snoop Dogg for his first single, a track from the movie *Deep Cover*, which was followed by *The Chronic*. This album was notable for the G-funk sound that would become a hallmark of hip-hop in the 1990s. G-funk uses funk music, artificially lowered tempos, hypnotic grooves, baselines that shake windows (and can be heard for city blocks), and multilayered synthesizes. *The Chronic* became multi-platinum and earned a Grammy for Dr. Dre for "Let Me Ride." Dre's friendship and collaboration with Snoop Dogg continued to grow, with Dre producing "Doggystyle," which debuted at number 1 on Billboard in 1993.

In 1996 Dr. Dre made a decision to leave Death Row Records, a decision that many say saved not just his career and credibility, but also his life. Suge Knight was developing Tupac Shakur into the industry's top artist, but Dre believed Suge Knight was too power-crazy and corrupt. His

departure turned out to be a good move because Tupac ended up murdered (after being shot on two separate occasions), and never was paid the
reported $17 million in royalties Knight owed him at the time of death,
and Knight ended up doing prison time.

So Dre left and started his own label, Aftermath Entertainment, and
released in 1996 *Dr. Dre Presents the Aftermath*, with the lead song "Been
There Done That" meant to indicate that his gangsta, violence-riddled
past was largely behind him, though he would return to it lyrically in the
future.

Though he was coming into his own as a producer, businessman, and
artist, sales for his label were struggling, until Dr. Dre discovered a new
talent who would change the course of his own life and the course of
rap—Marshall Mathers—and signed him to Aftermath in 1998. Mathers,
better known as Eminem, was part of the reason Dre won the Grammy for
Producer of the Year in 2000.

Eminem was quite the find for Dr. Dre and Aftermath. Growing up
in Detroit after being born in Missouri, Eminem was rapping as a teen
in clubs, footage of which has appeared on MTV and VH1. Though he
dropped out of school at age 17 because of truancy, he was a major force
in the predominantly black rap underground. He had a small-time record
deal for his first album and was washing dishes while trying to help raise his
young daughter in his often contentious relationship with his soon-to-be
ex-wife, whom he would later reconcile with—and split from again.

Jimmy Iovine of Interscope played a copy of Eminem's demo for Dr. Dre,
and in 1999 the pair released Eminem's *The Slim Shady LP*, a breakthrough
work of violent and sexual lyrics that was as criticized for its lyrics as it was
critically praised for its artistic value. Fans responded to the white rapper,
pushing the album to triple platinum status in less than a year. Critics
from Billboard praised the album while calling the lyrics "brutal" because
of the graphic violence. Parents and Christian groups protested, but the
publicity ended up bringing Eminem to a wider audience and pushed sales
even higher.

Eminem only went higher from there, as 2000's *The Marshall Mathers
LP* sold 1.76 million copies its first week, breaking Britney Spears's "Baby
One More Time" record for solo artist album sales and Snoop Dogg's record for fastest-selling hip-hop album. Eminem had his own eye for talent,
and he and Dr. Dre signed hard-core gangsta rapper 50 Cent to a recording
contract. Eminem also starred in the semiautobiographical movie *8-Mile*
in 2002. His movie work since then has included only a cameo, and aside
from 50 Cent, he has had little comparative success with Shady, his label
under Dre's company. Eminem has endured a multimillion-dollar slan-

der suit from his own mother and has remarried—and divorced a second time—the mother of his daughter.

In 2005, amid legal, family, and other personal problems, the high-octane Eminem was artistically stalled and took a break to regroup, spend more time with his daughter, and write more music. A new album has been rumored to be in the works for several years and is expected to be released in 2009.

HIP-HOP'S ROUGHEST ERA:
FROM TUPAC TO KANYE

Tupac Shakur, born in 1971 in New York City's East Harlem area of Manhattan, was originally a roadie and backup dancer for the hip-hop group Digital Undergound. As a solo artist, he began rapping about his life growing up in the ghetto amid violence and poverty in ghettos.

His mother, Afeni Shakur, was a Black Panther Party member in the 1960s and 1970s. She gave birth to Tupac just a month after getting acquitted on 150 charges of "conspiracy against the U.S. Government" and New York–area landmarks. Tupac showed artistic talent from a young age, and in high school, after his mother moved him to Maryland, he studied acting at the Baltimore School for the Arts. He also studied poetry, jazz, and ballet. He acted in the school's productions of Shakespeare and *The Nutcracker*. Though he could not afford the fashionable clothes his classmates had, he was popular, and his fellow students loved listening to rap. He became close friends with Jada Pinkett, who would go onto marry "lite" rapper Will Smith. In 1988 Shakur's mother moved them to Marin City, California, where he joined a local theater company to pursue acting. His mother's crack addiction led Tupac to move into a friend's house, though eventually he dropped out of high school.

He also rapped about drug abuse. His debut album was *2Pacalypse Now*, a play on the violent Vietnam movie *Apocalypse Now*. In 1991 Tupac was becoming a major player in hip-hop and rap. Tupac's troubles with the law became intense that year. In October of 1991, he sued the Oakland Police Department after claiming they beat him for jaywalking and settled the case for $42,000. Two years later, in 1993, in Atlanta, Tupac shot a pair of off-duty police officers who were harassing a black motorist. One officer was hit in the leg and the other in the buttocks. But charges against Tupac were dropped when it was publicized that the officers were intoxicated and had on them stolen weapons from a police evidence lockup.

While awaiting the verdict of a sexual assault charge against him in 1994, Tupac was robbed and shot five times, including twice in the head, outside of a recording studio in Manhattan, New York, and he accused Sean "Diddy" Combs, Andre Smalls, and Biggie Smalls, aka Notorious B.IG.

Tupac was later convicted of three charges, though not the most serious charges he was facing. In February 1995, he began serving his prison sentence for a sexual assault conviction, and though he was in prison, his album *Me Against the World* was released and went to number 1 for five weeks on the Billboard 100. With his case on appeal, Tupac was released from prison after serving 11 months of his 18-month sentence, with the $1.4 million put up by Death Row records CEO Suge Knight, who as a condition would have Tupac release three albums.

Tupac released the double album *All Eyez on Me* as the first and second albums of his deal with Suge. The double album was a departure from Tupac's previous introspective and reflective albums, going mostly "gangsta" and thug, though it sold nine million copies. Death Row was constantly embroiled in external and internal "beefs," with Dr. Dre leaving. On September 7, 1996, Tupac attended a Mike Tyson fight, at the MGM Grand in Las Vegas, Nevada. A member of the Crips gang was spotted in the hotel lobby after the fight, and Shakur rushed over and knocked the alleged Crips gang member to the ground, with Suge and his group beating the alleged gang member. The attack, which was captured by security cameras, was payback for a Crips robbery of a Death Row entourage member at a Foot Locker store. Just after 11 p.m. that evening, Shakur was with Suge's group in a black BMW, and they were stopped by police on bicycles for loud music and no license plates. After the plates were retrieved from the trunk of the BMW and put on the vehicle, they pulled away, and just 10 minutes later, a four-door white Cadillac pulled up to Tupac's side, the passenger side, and fired at least a dozen shots almost point blank at Tupac. Suge was hit as well, but Tupac took four bullets. After being resuscitated and surviving several surgeries, Tupac died six days later of hemorrhaging, simply unable to overcome the internal bleeding and dying of respiratory failure and cardiac arrest.

The rumors about who shot Tupac far surpassed evidence. The *Los Angeles Times* would report later that Diddy was involved, only to retract the story. Biggie was thought to have strong ties to the Crips gang and was thus implicated by hearsay, including statements that Biggie had provided the gun and placed a bounty on Shakur, though none of that was ever substantiated, and Biggie was said by colleagues to be in New York the night of the shooting, working in a recording studio. Some believe Suge orchestrated the whole thing because he owed Tupac $17 million in royalties, but nothing to sustain that has ever been produced as evidence.

ANOTHER LIFE CUT SHORT: BIGGIE SMALLS

The Notorious B.I.G. started out as Christopher Wallace. Like a lot of the most successful rappers of the 1990s, Biggie was from a New York City neighborhood, and in his case, it was Brooklyn's Bedford-Stuyvesant neighborhood. Surrounded by drugs and violence, just a couple of years after getting the nickname "Big," he began dealing drugs as a 12-year-old among the crack epidemic of that era. His mother, a preschool teacher who had Jamaican heritage—as did a lot of the more significant players in the origins of hip-hop—raised him alone after Biggie's father left when Biggie was just two years old.

Despite his extracurricular activities selling drugs, Biggie was a stand-out English student in middle school, even gaining honors in English. Biggie was already rapping by that point, having started as a kid with local groups such as The Techniques and the Old Gold Brothers.

Biggie did not like the Catholic high school he was attending and transferred to the now-famous rap-haven George Westinghouse Information Technology High School, where the student body included Jay-Z and Busta Rhymes. But Biggie lost interest in school and dropped out at age 17, and his criminal activity increased. An arrest in 1989 on weapons charges resulted in only probation, but that was revoked the next year on a violation. He got out again but in 1991 was busted in North Carolina for selling crack. Before making bail, he served nine months in a North Carolina prison. Once he got out, he went from being known as "big" to Biggie Smalls, inspired by the name of a gangster in the 1975 movie *Let's Do it Again*. Biggie made a demo tape, which arrived in the hands of DJ Mister Cee, who passed it along to hip-hop magazine *The Source*, which gave Biggie's demo a very positive review. That review drew the attention of Sean "Diddy" Combs (then known as "Puffy"), who signed Biggie to a recording deal. Biggie continued to sell drugs until Combs found out and told Biggie he had to stop. Additionally, Combs was striking out on his own, leaving Uptown to start his own label that would go onto great success, Bad Boy, and he took the new signee with him. From there, the six-foot-tall, nearly 400-pound Biggie underwent another name change, becoming Notorious B.I.G.; he debuted in 1993 on a couple of Mary Blige tracks and cut a song for the movie *Who's the Man?* Finally, in September 1994, Biggie's first album, *Ready to Die*, was released, spawning the hit single "Juicy."

That fall, Biggie married talented artist Faith Evans, who was on the same label with Combs. Two months after *Ready to Die* was released, Tupac was shot and accused both his onetime buddy Biggie and Combs of being behind it.

This was the heyday of the hip-hop wars and the bloodiest, most deadly time in music.

Combs's East Coast label Bad Boy was challenging Suge Knight's Tupac-led West Coast Death Row record for bragging and sales rights.

Biggie continued to work hard that year, and in 1995, with *Ready to Die* still hot on the charts, Biggie worked with Michael Jackson and R. Kelly, establishing Biggie as one of the most powerful new artists in the music industry. But trouble also had a line on Biggie, with one assault charge levied by a concert promoter at one point and another filed by a pair of fans who claimed Biggie came after them with a baseball bat after they sought autographs.

And in 1996 Biggie's legal woes got worse, starting with a raid at Biggie's New Jersey home that turned up weapons and marijuana. He also became involved with up-and-coming artist Lil' Kim, and Tupac not only became involved with Faith Evans, to whom Biggie was still legally married, but also rapped about it on his next album, further fanning the flames of the feud. Biggie's work on his second album was interrupted when he suffered serious injuries in a car accident that required him to be in a wheelchair. Later, in September 1996, Tupac was slain in Las Vegas, and though no charges or evidence was ever produced linking Biggie to the killing, rumors were everywhere. Biggie drew the ire of critics when he chose not to attend a hip-hop antiviolence summit in Harlem after Tupac was killed. Faith Evans gave birth to Biggie's son on October 29, 1996.

Biggie never got to see his son grow up and never got to make it right with Faith Evans or follow through with Lil' Kim. Nor did he get to pursue his music. He went to the West Coast, and on March 9, 1997, in Los Angeles, was leaving a *Vibe* magazine party at the Petersen Automotive Museum, an event that included Faith Evans, Combs, and members of the Bloods and Crips gangs.

Biggie was in the front passenger seat, and his bodyguard was driving, with a member of Biggie's protégé group, Junior M.A.F.I.A., in the back seat. Biggie's vehicle was being followed by another SUV carrying Combs and three bodyguards. When Biggie's SUV stopped at a stoplight, a vehicle pulled up on Biggie's side and sprayed 10 shots into the vehicle; Biggie was hit four times in the chest. He was pronounced dead within a half hour at Cedars-Sinai Medical Center.

Just weeks after his death, at the end of March, Biggie's album *Life After Death* was released, as planned; it sold 700,000 units in its first week and spent four weeks at number 1 on the charts.

Though Kanye West was not a player in the industry at that point, he turned 20 years old in 1997, had dropped out of college (twice), and was trying to break into the hip-hop industry. This was the violent, blood-spattered industry he was about to step into. Those around him had to have concern that Kanye, who had no affiliation with gangs, drugs, or violence—the only annoying thing he had done at that point was work for telemarketing firms—was stepping out to chase his dreams into a business that had become a nightmare.

Chapter 8

KANYE'S "BIG BROTHER" JAY-Z

Though Jay-Z is widely and correctly regarded as Kanye West's mentor, Jay-Z is only a few years older than Kanye. Born Shawn Corey Carter on December 4, 1969, Jay-Z is now married to Beyoncé Knowles, a successful artist who was part of Destiny's Child before launching her solo career.

Unlike Kanye, Jay-Z is from New York. Though Jay-Z does not appear to be as "street" as 50 Cent, Jay-Z can certainly hold his own. He was raised in Brooklyn's infamous Marcy Houses, a housing project, by his mother after his father took off when Jay-Z and his brother were little.[1]

Jay-Z was a student at Eli Whitney High School, with fellow student and eventual rapper AZ, until the school was closed. From there, Jay-Z went on to a high school in downtown Brooklyn that at the time included the Notorious B.I.G. and Busta Rhymes. Jay-Z then gave a third high school, this time one in New Jersey, a try but again did not graduate. Though he was never arrested for it, Jay-Z said he was too caught up in selling drugs to finish school.[2]

His nickname has several roots. He was first dubbed "Jazzy" by friends in the neighborhood for his musical inclinations, and his mentor musically was Jaz-O, and there was also a "J/Z" rail service that had a stop in Marcy. Jay-Z actually did some work on Jaz-O records in the 1980s and early 1990s. Jay-Z's break as a solo artist came when he freestyled against rapper Zai, catching the eye of music executives. His first formal rap single and video was the song "I Can't Get with That." Though it was done on his own, he was tired of not having a deal, and he struck out with Dame Dash and Kareem Biggs to form Roc-A-Fella Records.[3]

Roc-A-Fella records, and the Roc-A-Fella brand, are some of the great grassroots success stories for not just hip-hop but brand development too.

The first album for Jay-Z on Roc-A-Fella was *Reasonable Doubt* in 1996, and with Roc-A-Fella at that time still an independent label, it did not reach a wide audience, though it did receive a lot of critical praise. Def Jam saw potential in the label and in Jay-Z and in 1997 bought 50 percent of Roc-A-Fella, for what turned out to be a bargain price of $1.5 million.[4]

Dash and Jay-Z also moved into theaters with Rocafella Films and into clothing with Rocafella Wear. Though Jay-Z is the fashion face of most of Roc-A-Fella's ventures, Dame Dash was a big part of the company's success. In late 2004, Def Jam bought the remaining 50 percent of Roc-A-Fella. Dame Dash and Jay-Z parted ways at that time, and though Dame started his own label, Kanye West and most of the other Roc-A-Fella artists stayed with Jay-Z. The pair had a final falling-out over the other business interests of Roc-A-Fella, and in 2006 Jay-Z took over the clothing line they had started. In 2007, Jay-Z sold the Roc-A-Fella brand to Iconix Brand Group for more than $200 million—after buying out Dash for $30 million—and remains attached to the brand in somewhat of a consulting role, with some oversight for marketing and product development. The influx of cash has made Jay-Z a major player in entertainment economics, and he owns a share of the NBA's New Jersey Jets and the popular club franchise the 40/40 Club. Jay-Z's next big deal was the reported $150 million with Live Nation, which also signed Madonna and Shakira. Jay-Z's deal with Live Nation pays him that incredible sum to, for 10 years, run a record label, a talent and management agency, and a music publishing company.[5]

Kanye will always be indebted to Dash, who was the one who believed Kanye's preppy image and lack of street edge would not impede him as a hip-hop artist. Dash will also always be linked to Jay-Z, who, when Jay-Z could not find a record deal, took it upon himself to make Jay-Z's initial CD, even borrowing a boat to film Jay-Z's video. Jay-Z was trying to break in during a tough time for East Coast hip-hop artists because the West Coast crew of Dr. Dre, Snoop Dogg, and Tupac were ruling the hip-hop business and dominating the charts with hit after hit, and they were developing new artists at a far better and more successful rate, at the time, than their East Coast counterparts. When Dash finally ended up agreeing to a buyout from Roc-A-Fella over creative differences with Jay-Z, in particular what ventures should be pursued by the company, it was the end of an era. The deal breaker was, according to *New York Magazine,* when Dame Dash offered artist Cam'ron, of whom Jay-Z was not a big fan, his own label without Jay-Z being consulted. Jay-Z won big-time financially and in terms of taking control of the company, and Dame Dash quickly went into purgatory. Cam'ron, who landed at Warner, cut a track in 2006 that took a ton of shots at Jay-Z for taking the label and all the properties associated with it, but Jay-Z just laughed and kept producing hits on his own and developing more success for the artists at Roc-A-Fella, including his most accomplished protégé, Kanye.[6]

MENTOR DASH'S UGLY EXIT

Several of Dash's recent and late Roc-A-Fella moves did not pan out. Victoria Beckham, also known as "Posh Spice" from the Spice Girls, did a double-single which Dash produced and that charted at number 3 in England, but it was never released on an album because of controversy over Beckham becoming an "urban" sort of artist after a career in pop music. Dash's successes post-Roc have been in producing a movie, his second, and his deals with an alcoholic beverage producer and a watch maker.

Dash did get his own label with Def Jam after selling his interest in Roc-A-Fella; however, the success he had with Roc-A-Fella has not followed him to Dame Dash Music Group, which he started with the other co-founder of Roc-A-Fella, Kareem Biggs. All four artists they originally signed to Dash's new venture eventually left, including Beanie Sigel, with whom Kanye worked when he first joined Roc-A-Fella as a producer. Dash told *New York Magazine* that he does have more deals in the works. However, success has eluded Dash since he parted ways with Roc-A-Fella. Dash dated rising R&B music star Aliayah—who sold 32 million albums in her short career—until her death in a plane crash in the Bahamas in 2001. Dash then married fashion designer Rachel Roy, and they have two children together. Dash also has diabetes and does charitable work to support research into treatments and potential cures.[7]

Though Jay-Z's first non-independent label album, basically a re-release of what he had done on his own, *Reasonable Doubt*, hit only number 23 on the charts, it received critical praise and was notable for having the Notorious B.I.G. on one of the tracks. Another boost came from Sean "P. Diddy" Combs, who produced Jay-Z's second album, *In My Lifetime, Volume I*, in 1997. Jay-Z had a distribution deal with Priority that would get the album into more retail outlets, though he completed the well-produced album with a heavy heart, given that Biggie (Notorious B.I.G.) had been killed. He followed that in 1998 with *Vol. 2 . . . Hard Knock Life*, which sold more than eight million copies, and 1999's *Vol. 3, Life and Times of S. Carter*, which sold 5.6 million units. Along the way he was working with and helping develop such talent as Timbaland and had a hit with Ja Rule. Showing how he planned to develop as a music executive and overall cultural icon, Jay-Z produced an album of Roc-A-Fella signees in 2000, *The Dynasty: Roc La Familia*, and though it generated a lot of criticism, it sold 2 million units.

In 2001 Jay-Z, who was deep in the process of developing talented artists and producers, decided to work with a young upstart named Kanye West on Jay-Z's forthcoming double album, *The Blueprint: The Gift & The Curse*, though it experienced more success when it was pared down into half the tracks of the original and sold under the title *The Blueprint 2.1. Blueprint 2.1* had one hit single after another, including "Excuse Me Miss" and "03 Bonnie and Clyde," the latter of which included his then-girlfriend (and now wife) Beyoncé. Lenny Kravitz contributed to the hit track "Guns & Roses," "Hovi Baby" became another radio hit from the album, and "The Dream" included contributions from Faith Evans and the Notorious B.I.G. But it was the song "The Bounce" that would springboard relative newcomer Kanye West into the hip-hop scene as a major player, albeit at the time still largely as a talented producer.

Jay-Z is also well known for his heated rivalry—also called a "beef"—with fellow successful hip-hop artist Nas. Though harsh words were exchanged, often through rap lyrics, the two came together when Jay-Z signed Nas to a deal with Def Jam, of which Jay-Z was CEO. He contributed to Nas's album on the song "Black Republican," and their "beef" was largely regarded as, though genuine, a boost in publicity at the time of sagging hip-hop CD sales. Jay-Z followed in 2003 with the *Black Album*, which sold three million copies, and Jay-Z toured with onetime rival 50 Cent and former schoolmate Busta Rhymes. Jay-Z's 2004 album, *Collision Course*, sold more than 2 million copies. In October 2005, Jay-Z put on the "I Declare War" concert, raising fans' expectations that Jay-Z was out to settle an old score or start a new one. However, on a stage with a mockup of the White House's Oval Office, he officially ended his beef with Nas and included a star-filled lineup of Roc-A-Fella's current and former artists, including Kanye West, who by then was the hottest thing in hip-hop, and maybe in all genres of music.[8]

Jay-Z followed in 2006 with the album *Kingdom Come* and in 2007 with *American Gangster* and continued to sell millions of each release. He continues to have business interests outside of recording; he announced he would step down as the head of Def Jam Records to pursue other interests and is involved in everything from multimillion dollar real estate ventures and clothing.

When Kanye West showed up in New York at Roc-A-Fella, he was wearing Italian shoes, medium-sized T-shirts that looked tailored, and not sagging pants that showed his underwear, but fashion-savvy pants that made him look more like a businessman.

"Kanye wore a pink shirt with the collar sticking up and Gucci loafers," Dash, then Roc-A-Fella CEO, said. "It was obvious we were not from the same place or cut from the same cloth."[9]

Even Jay-Z was caught off-guard by West's appearance.

"Yo, I don't think this is gonna work right here," West told MTV about what he thought Jay-Z was thinking at their initial meeting.[10]

Jay-Z remembers Kanye's clothes were only part of the difference—he also did not have the background of living in projects or a life in crime as a backdrop to a potential recording career.

"We all grew up street guys who had to do whatever we had to do to get by," Jay-Z said. "Then there's Kanye, who to my knowledge has never hustled a day in his life. I didn't see how it could work."[11]

But Dame Dash spoke up, saying Kanye could be hip-hop's version of Babyface. Sprinkle in Jay-Z and Cam'ron, and the music had the backing of the hip-hop elite.

West's own songs have not been about life on the streets or life on the run from the law. His songs have been about his own life. He rhymed about the time his grandmother almost died. He raps about the "death diamond" mines around the world. He has rapped compassionately about AIDs and about how little has been done to fight what is perceived as a disease that affects the minority community more than it does white America.

When Dame Dash left Roc-A-Fella, Kanye had a choice and could have followed Dash. But he stuck with Jay-Z, and when some called him out for leaving the guy who gave him his start, West admitted freely that it could come across as disloyal. But by that time, West's relationship with Jay-Z had developed on so many levels, especially as a music venture, that West thought this fork in the road left only the obvious choice of moving forward with Roc-A-Fella. West said when Dame Dash and Jay-Z split, it was like enduring a divorce of sorts. Though both had been mentors, West was stuck in the middle and had to make a choice that was best for his own future.

Jay-Z has been more than a mentor. In fact, Jay-Z has been the measuring stick that Kanye is constantly judging himself against while trying to become better. He admits he writes with the idea of beating Jay-Z's next best effort.

"I feel like a spoiled kid," West said, "someone who's got a little scooter hooked up to a generator that powers a city."[12]

But West is true to himself and his music—and by extension of those factors, to his fans—even if it comes at the expense of Jay-Z. This actually happened on the song "We Major," when Kanye used Nas, who is Jay-Z's nemesis, on the track without Jay-Z's knowledge. Nas is one of West's idols, and West said that was something he had to do to be true to himself.

After he survived the life-changing car crash (see chapter 9), which was much more serious than first reported, Kanye found himself at a crossroads in his life. He knew he had been given a second chance and felt that God was giving him the opportunity to have a positive effect on people. And although he puts himself atop the hip-hop community at times, he says he is never doing it at the expense of putting others down. He simplifies it by saying that if something is good, it is good and stands on its own merits, that if it cannot stand on its own merits, it does not deserve further discussion. He included Nas because he found the hip-hop artist's involvement on "We Major" to be something that inspired people. He also had a personal mission, to bridge the rift between Jay-Z and Nas, two of hip-hop's biggest superstars.

Another of Kanye's memorable collaborations was with Maroon 5 lead singer Adam Levine, who has worked with, among others, country music's Sara Evans. When Kanye was on his way to an awards show in Rome—a show where West would have one of his famous outbursts after not winning—West played the song for Levine as the two sat in first class for the plane ride over to Italy. The song was slated to be on West's next album. After listening to the song, Levine said he thought the song sounded like one he had written but was unsure if Maroon 5 would record it because it sounded too R&B. Kanye suggested Levine work with him on the track, and it became another of Kanye West's hits that crossed genres and brought new audiences to West's sound, as well as giving Levine a chance to continue to stretch himself as a an artist outside of Maroon 5. Kanye said Levine's contribution was magical, and it even felt like God had had a hand in getting Levine into the studio and in Levine's performance.[13]

Kanye has said that the best music comes from pain and all the experiences that one has in life, which shape people into who they are. West knows all eyes are on him, and he readily admits to being nervous. In interviews he has compared going onstage to what magicians must feel like, waiting for the stunt to fail, for the trick to backfire, for the spectacle of failure.[14]

NOTES

1. Eric Konigsberg. "Why Damon Dash Hates Mondays." *New York Magazine*, June 12, 2006, http://nymag.com/news/profiles/17268/.

2. Charlie Rose. "Interview with Jay-Z." *Charlie Rose*, PBS, November 9, 2007.

3. Simon Vozick-Levinson. "Jay-Z's Brotherly Love." Music Q&A. *Entertainment Weekly Online*, Fall 2007.

4. Eric Konigsberg. "Why Damon Dash Hates Mondays."

5. Hilary Cross. "Live Nation, Jay-Z Deal Imminent." *Billboard*, April 2, 2008.

6. Mark Ecko. "Future Shock." *Complex*, August–September, 2007.

7. Eric Konigsberg. "Why Damon Dash Hates Mondays."

8. Associated Press. "Kanye West Jams with Nas, John Legend." June 23, 2006.

9. Josh Tyrangiel. "Why You Can't Ignore Kanye." *Time*, August 21, 2005.

10. Sway Calloway. "All Eyes on Kanye West." MTV.com, August 18, 2005.

11. Josh Tyrangiel. "Why You Can't Ignore Kanye."

12. Chris Norris. "Top of the World." *Blender*, September 2005.

13. Sway Calloway. "All Eyes on Kanye West."

14. Ibid.

Chapter 9

FROM PRODUCER TO ARTIST

Kanye West first had success as a producer for such artists as Jay-Z, Alicia Keyes, and Beyoncé. He produced Jay-Z and Beyoncé's "03 Bonnie & Clyde," Keyes's "You Don't Know my Name," and Beanie Sigel's "The Truth."

When Kanye was behind the scenes, only a dozen or so people were aware of who he was, whereas as an artist, soon the whole world would know him. Being the artist also brings an enormous amount of pressure compared to producing, because it is his name and face that are out there, whereas to the general public, the producer—though it is a very serious and important role—is merely a name on the liner notes.

The practical side of being an artist also became an issue. Kanye had never had to worry about signing autographs or being recognized when he went out in public. He developed a routine where he would cover his head and feign a headache to be able to go out shopping and not be stopped. It's an issue that Kanye actually asked Ludacris about the first time Kanye was in the studio with him. Kanye had wondered where a star as big as Ludacris went when he wanted to go out to do something simple like get dinner or see a movie. Ludacris said such excursions were something West would have to learn to do without because even places frequented by "white people" would include patrons who would recognize West.

West has a lot of passion not just for the music, but also for how it is presented, both as a producer and with his videos. He is consumed with the art direction of projects. He admits that with his goals for his own label, a lot of issues present themselves. He knows this firsthand because he had to work with so many talented artists in the first place just to be able to work on his own material. That is one of the many reasons he takes his losses so personally at awards shows, whether it's the Grammy for a song he wrote and produced or an award for a video he brought to life from his imagination. As an artist, his first two albums brought home an eye-popping six Grammys. He takes offense to being called arrogant when he claims he is just being honest. He points out that when he said Justin Timberlake deserved to win at the Grammys, he was not being humble— just honest, just as he had been when he said his honest belief was that he deserved to win at other times. He was, in other words, just stating his opinion of what the best work done was that particular year, and he was revealing the truths he had come to, not trying to be either humble or tactless.

"When people come up to you, like, 'That was really good,' you're sup-posed to play stupid, like, 'Wow, you really think so?' Because people can't really handle the truth," West said. "But I am the truth. I'd rather be hated for what I am than loved for what I'm not."[1]

Sean Daly of the *St. Petersburg Times* calls West "pathologically hon-est." In a world where comments are spun away from the truth, and artists are more worried about their public relations image than true feelings, many happen to find Kanye's frankness refreshing. It would be better— and even Kanye would point this out—at times if he could not react when he initially feels even a hint of disrespect. But his reactions are still hon-est, and that he wears his heart on his sleeve portends a certain integrity to media members such as Daly.[2]

West says he has more talent as a producer—someone who can draw a bunch of effects, sometimes unlikely matches, together, and make sense of them—than he has as an artist. He is tireless in postproduction, doing dozens of remixes of songs and changing things around, trying something new, and adding or subtracting certain things. Jay-Z was stunned when West was on tour and sent back more than a dozen versions of a track Kanye was working on for an upcoming album.

In October 2002, not long after knowing he was on the verge of record-ing his own record after a slew of producing successes, Kanye was involved in a serious car accident that would impact the rest of his life. Kanye had fallen asleep at the wheel at about 4 a.m. in his rented Lexus in Los An-geles.[3] He hit another car, breaking the legs of that driver. Kanye's jaw was broken in three places. He had what he called nasal fractures—to the point where if he started to talk, his nose would bleed. He had to have his jaw wired shut so that it could heal. He called the days following the accident the most pain he has felt in his life, something he would not wish upon even his worst enemy. He was worried about having surgery, and because his injuries affected his breathing, he thought back to horror stories about people dying during even simple surgeries. He was bleeding profusely from the mouth, and doctors and nurses had to use suction to constantly remove the pooling blood and mucus. Kanye actually talked to his mother on his cell phone as rescue workers were trying to cut the car apart so that he could be removed. He just wanted to let his mother know he was all right.[4]

To make matters worse, the distressed West felt at the scene like he was getting less than acceptable medical care because of being black, with police testing him more than once for his blood-alcohol level even though he said he was not drinking before driving. The Los Angeles Police Department countered that administering at least three sobriety tests is standard procedure on driving-under-the-influence suspects, especially someone like Kanye who was at fault in the accident, but West's point is that in his medical condition, any more than one test was too much. He was questioned at the scene, he says, and kept asking them to get him to the hospital because he was in such pain.

"I was sitting in the car after the accident, and they kept asking me questions," West said. "I was just telling them, 'I want to go to the hospital, I'm in so much pain right now. I'm gagging on blood right now.' I was just trying to breathe. Then they finally put one of them hard-ass neck braces on me, and it hurt. Then they put me on the stretcher, and it was on some *Something About Mary* because they dropped me, and I hit my head and jaw."[5] (In the movie *Something About Mary*, actor Ben Stiller's character is treated harshly and carelessly as he is loaded into an ambulance.)

After Kanye was taken to the hospital, he said his jaw was wired shut incorrectly and had to be re-broken and reset properly. Rather than let the whole accident and resulting injuries get him down, West went on a prolific writing spree while he recovered. He had to learn how to pronounce words properly again, and he struggled at first with not slurring words. He was concerned that this would affect him as an artist and performer. After his hospital stay, he returned to the music studio two weeks later, rapping about the pain and hassles he had suffered in the accident and at the hospital, using a sample from Chaka Khan's hit "Through the Fire" as part of the track "Through the Wire."

"I feel like the album was my medicine," West said. "It would take my mind away from the pain—away from the dental appointments, from my teeth killing me, from my mouth being wired shut, from the fact that I looked like I just fought Mike Tyson. The record wouldn't have been as big without the accident—I nearly died. That's the best thing that can happen to a rapper."[6]

"Through the Wire," and the inspiration that was the car accident, only fused West's passion and creativity—and more literally, his jaw bones— together during what proved to be the pivotal point in his then-fledgling career. Had he not been so challenged, even he admits he might not have turned one of life's important corners with such verve and veracity.

"I was mad because I was not being taken seriously as a rapper for a long time," West said. "Whether it was because I didn't have a larger-than-life persona, or I was perceived as the guy who made beats, I was disrespected as a rapper. I was making good beats before I made good raps, but I've been rapping for longer. It's hard to rap, man. You can't accidentally rap well, but you can accidentally make a good beat. Accidents—weird, right? An accident changed my life."[7]

Though Kanye West's music includes words not often seen in the Bible or heard in church, the Christian is very passionate about his faith and says to discard him as a Christian simply because of profanity or what could be called cultural vulgarities would really miss who he is as a person. He is spiritual to his core, something not everyone realizes. The accident was further proof to him that he had to continue his prayers and faith.

"I think that God spared my life to make music and to help people, to always put out positive energy," West said. "One of the reasons why I don't have beef with any rapper or with anybody is because of the positive energy I put out. So even if I hold myself up, I'm not putting anybody else down."[8]

When West starts to get a feeling of déjà vu, it relaxes him, because he knows the direction he is headed in the right one. Spiritual by nature, and within his genre extremely spiritual, West has said that God has him on a specific path, that certain people are put into his life as he travels down his path.

KANYE UNPLUGGED

Although he is insistent about drawing positive attention to his work, Kanye West actually does not like to be interviewed. He has asked people at pre-release invite-only gatherings in fact to not even tell their friends when they leave about what he said or what the new songs are. His biggest fear is that his comments will be either taken out of context or used entirely in a different light.

"It's the way you edit me that reverts it to black and white," West told a reporter.[9]

West claims to speak in colors, not simply letters. His world of shapes and patterns does not translate well to linear thinkers, he maintains. He takes pride in giving comments and insights that are both edgy and spiritually connected, words that will inspire. He says in that context, he is able to translate himself, as a whole person, to others. However, he says the media chooses just quotes, and even parts of quotes, that distort not just his message, but his image.

Perhaps his insistence on context has something to do with his music, over which he has complete editorial and creative control. Reporters are prone to use his comments, he says, to fit their story, whether that presents an accurate perception of him or not. One person who did want to go on the record as a proud "big brother" was Jay-Z.

"It makes me proud as someone who's watched his growth from the beginning, when he came in as a hungry producer, to now he's a rock star," Jay-Z said. "I'm happy for him on that level. And I'm excited for creativity as well, because I think that's a win for that as well. You know, people mimic success. And in order to mimic that success, you have to put in a lot of work. You have to really care about the music."[10]

West takes great pride in being a hip-hop artist who can make songs that mean something, noting that in just 16 lines of verse, every single line has to have an impact. He says he has taken the lyrics and meaning to an entirely new level, particularly in terms of being poetic and philosophical. He admits the profane words are used just to add smoothness, but that the clever turns of a phrase, his originality, and his spirituality bring to his music a special quality that, before he became an artist, was lacking in his genre.

"I feel like my lyrics are—if not the—then equal to the realest lyrics out," Kanye said. "I connected with so many people without talking about guns and drugs—it's harder to go to work 365 days than shoot a person in one day [and] there's nothing about wearing a pink Polo that would make anyone believe that I would hold a gun."[11]

He went so far as to claim that he is no longer competing with hip-hop artists at this point, that he is more of an "ambassador" for the genre. He does not like that hip-hop, as a brand, has long been associated with bravado, bad dressing, and raps that are only about the artist, rather than what the audience cares about most. He takes pride that his songs provide inspiration and guidelines to help in everyday life.

That has put the "art" in the artist known as Kanye West. He is proud to have created a brand, not unlike the fashion designers or shoe companies who are built on quality, trend setting, and inspiration.

He and his publicist now turn down print interview requests, preferring broadcast only because Kanye is not edited down as severely in the electronic format compared to print.

"People who write stuff paraphrase," West said. "They take what I'm saying—and I speak in colors—and flip it to black and white. Sometimes, I might say something that has four or five meanings. If I'm being sarcastic, they'll take out the set up or the punch line and I sound like a jerk. It's the edit."[12]

Although West admits to having an ego, a lot of it is drawn out of his perfectionism and commitment to artistic integrity, qualities he is perhaps unsure those who are writing about him in print share. And although his ego does seem to take on a life of its own, he points out that having an ego is a healthy thing, something that can drive artists, and everyday people, to perform their best at work, at home, at church, and in relationships. West's justification is that his ego is not used to put others down. He is competing, in other words, against himself, though he would like it if people gave his work the appreciation and respect he believes it deserves. He enjoys feeling good about the music he creates.

NO MORE NASTINESS WITH NAS

The hip-hop artist Nas is one of those who has been in several "beefs" with various superstars in the industry.

Nasir Jones became known as Kid Wave and then Nasty Nas in the hip-hop world and is now just "Nas." Like several top hip-hop stars, he was raised in New York City's housing projects, calling the Queensbridge Housing Projects home while he was growing up, though he spent his youngest years in Brooklyn's Crown Heights, a neighborhood that endured a lot of racial strife through the decades.

Nas broke into rap with his neighbor, Willy "Ill Will" Graham. Together they met Queens-area producer William Mitchell, also known as the Large Professor. Nas and Graham worked together and were close several times to record deals, but Graham was shot and killed in Queensbridge in 1992. But MC Serch gave Nas a break, signing to manage him, which ultimately led to Nas signing with Columbia Records.

Like Kanye West years later, Nas's first album was seen both as groundbreaking and as an instant rap classic. *Illmatic*, which was released in 1994, had a group of successful MCs working with him on the album, including AZ and Q-Tip. Nas's father, successful jazz musician Olu Dara, also had a guest appearance on the album. The album was critically praised, but in an era where illegal music downloading had just caught on nationally, and there was little policing of such bootlegging, the CD did not bring in a huge number in terms of sales, though eventually it was certified platinum. Nas switched managers and went for more crossover appeal with his

1998 release, *It Was Written*, and had several hits. The album also marked the debut of an all-star hip-hop group, The Firm, which included Nas, AZ, Foxy Brown, and Cormega. The Firm signed with Dr. Dre but fired Cormega while working on its first album for Dre. That led Cormega to "beef" with Nas through several of Cormega's songs. The Firm did not survive long. The first album had slow sales initially, and the band split up to pursue their solo careers.

Nas got a boost on his next album, *I Am*, which seemed to be a cross between *Illmatic* and *It Was Written* as Diddy worked on a track with him called "Hate Me Now," which generated a whole new feud. Enlisting Diddy, critics of Nas claimed, showed that Nas was a commercial sellout. A spoof video was done and aired on MTV by Hype Williams that showed Diddy and Nas being crucified. Diddy and his bodyguards took it beyond the lyrical page and went to the office of Steve Stoute, who directed the video, and allegedly broke a bottle on Stoute's head. The case was later settled. Trying to gather songs pirated from *I Am* to re-release as the album *Nastradamus* hit several snags, causing several delays. Nas insisted on re-cording new material, pushing the release date back, and the 1999 release of *Nastradamus* barely caused a blip on the music world's radar, producing only one minor hit.

In 2001 Nas was supposed to record with Jay-Z on the mogul's "Dead Presidents" track off *Reasonable Doubt*. The two hip-hop artists exchanged a series of barbs through lyrics. On Jay-Z's album *Blueprint*, which Kanye West contributed to, Jay-Z took another swipe at Nas, with a line that basically said Nas was only good for one hit song every 10 years. Nas shot back with biting lyrics at Jay-Z and Tupac. Nas, in the Biggie camp— Tupac and Biggie were the first big public rivals in rap—kept going back and forth with Jay-Z.

Finally, the feud ended in 2005, during a Jay-Z event called "I De-clare War," which actually became a peace summit for the rap world. Nas joined Jay-Z onstage for "Dead Presidents," and the two went on in fol-lowing months to collaborate for a song on each one's next album.

Kanye has always called Jay-Z his most significant musical advocate, but also says Nas is one of his "idols," and he has worked with both on recent tracks.

In fact, on *Graduation*, West does a tribute song to Jay-Z called "Big Brother" that, for all the good things he raps about Jay-Z, he has some hurt included for how Jay-Z treated him at times. But that, West said, is what makes it genuine; although the hip-hop world is not always one big happy family, it is still one family. He said Jay-Z never said a negative word about the unflattering parts of "Big Brother." He said uniting Jay-Z and Nas on his CDs is a tribute to the impressive contribution both have made to the industry.

"Let me tell you this, we made this like Jay's favorite song on the album," Kanye said. "So the thing is, when something is so good, you can't deny it. When you hear the horns on 'We Major,' and you hear the chorus come in, and you hear Nas, that could like warm somebody's heart. Good music can break through anything and maybe start to break down the wall between two of the greatest MCs that we have."[13]

Nas had also had a beef with 50 Cent, claiming Fiddy didn't do "real" music. Fiddy, of course, responded, taking a shot at Nas's wife Kelis. Nas additionally made news in 2008 by writing a song going after FOX News commentator Bill O'Reilly. The album was supposed to have a single-word title—the N word—but the label refused to let that stand as the title, and public opinions weighed in heavily against Nas from the likes of Al Sharpton and Jesse Jackson. Major retail outlets also said they would not carry it if the N-word was used for the title. So it was changed to "Untitled."

KANYE STAYS "IN SYNC" WITH POP MUSIC

If there is someone who mirrors Kanye West musically and in fashion—and in terms of breaking down barriers for hits—surely that person would be Justin Timberlake.

Timberlake, though, had a much more formal training and background to prepare for the Grammy-winning solo career he has had. Timberlake's public music career was jumpstarted when he, along with eventual 'N Sync member JC Chasez, Britney Spears, and Christina Aguilera, won a role on Disney's Mickey Mouse Club. Justin also had a brief appearance on Star Search.

But he became a part of pop culture as a member of 'N Sync, which, along with the Backstreet Boys, was one of the most successful acts put together by Lou Perlman, who is now in federal prison on fraud charges.

Like Kanye, Timberlake is originally from the South, born in Memphis, Tennessee, a place that would be very near to Kanye's heart as it relates to Dr. Martin Luther King. Like Kanye, Justin is a Christian but professes, as does Kanye, to be more spiritual than into organized religion.

'N Sync hit in 1995, when Justin was just 14, and had a string of hits overseas before developing a teeny-bop fan frenzy in the United States. Songs such as "Tearin' Up My Heart" and "It's Gonna Be Me" helped 'N Sync sell more than 50 million albums before they broke up in 2002.

While all the 'N Sync members struck out on their own, only one struck gold, Timberlake. His first album, *Justified*, debuted in the second spot on the charts and eventually sold 3 million copies, and a name familiar to West fans, Timbaland, helped lend a strong R&B flavor to Timberlake's solo sound that gave the album life well into 2003, with hits that included "Cry Me a River."

From there, Timberlake built his brand, and his income from outside music shot through the roof. His track "I'm Lovin' It" was bought by fast-food giant McDonald's, which used it in its highly successful "I'm Lovin' It" campaign, a deal that brought Timberlake a reported $6 million.

He also found controversy in 2004, not by saying anything about the president like West, but by ripping off a piece of material from Janet Jackson's dress during a halftime performance in Super Bowl XXXVIII, and it was Justin who, in an apology, first used the now much-imitated phrase "wardrobe malfunction." In an artistic twist, he was going to be banned from the Grammys, but instead showed up and read a scripted apology and then walked off with two Grammy wins.

Timberlake's collaborations have also been very successful, both commercially and critically, including his Grammy-nominated rap with the Black Eyed Peas, "Where Is the Love?"

Like Jay-Z, Justin has a lot going on outside of music. Justin's work includes a fashion deal with label William Rast and several restaurants. Like Kanye with Jay-Z, Timberlake has a strong working relationship with an icon in his own genre, Madonna. In addition to touring extensively, Timberlake has also received critical praise for his roles in several movies, and he did the voice of the king in the third Shrek installment.

West has a lot of respect for Timberlake, whose 2006 sensation, *Sexy-Back*, further established the Timberlake brand in both music and fashion and further cemented Timberlake's status as a budding cultural icon.

"My biggest inspiration and biggest competition is Justin Timberlake, he's the only other person that gets an across-the-board response and respect level black radio, white radio," West said. "If Justin hadn't come out and killed the game, I can't say that my album, singles and videos would be on the same level that they're on. We push each other. I look at me and Justin, like Prince and Michael Jackson in their day."[14]

In November 2006, Kanye was the opening act for U2 and their Vertigo Tour. He also opened for the Rolling Stones, a brave move considering Justin Timberlake had opened for the Stones in Toronto and was booed so mercilessly that Mick Jagger and Keith Richards had to come out and insist that the audience stop heckling Justin and stop throwing water bottles and other objects at the stage. West suffered no such difficulties opening for either legendary band and brought his brand of music to a whole new audience; indeed, it is hard to imagine another hip-hop artist opening for such classic rock bands.

Timberlake started his own record label and has worked with a producer who helped Kanye do some of his best work, Rick Rubin.

Rubin is another key player in not just Kanye's career, but hip-hop overall, and the dots connect all the way to Jay-Z. Def Jam was founded by Rubin, who would go onto work with Kanye later in Rubin's career. Rubin started Def Jam while he was a student at New York University. The Jewish New York native played in a band, Hose, and in 1982 released Def Jam's first single, a small 45 rebounds-per-minute vinyl record that was packaged in a brown paper bag, with no label. Rubin, a guitar player in his punk band, sought to get more involved in New York City's hip-hop music scene. In 1983 he produced on Def Jam with DJ Jazzy Jay the single "It's Yours" for hip-hop artist T La Rock, and with distributor help, he was able to sell the record worldwide.

Rubin's hip-hop career took off when Jazzy Jay introduced Rubin to Russell Simmons at a New York City nightclub. Simmons joined Def Jam, and he and Rubin pushed out Jazzy Jay. Their first effort together in 1984 was LL Cool J's single "I Need a Beat," and then Rubin signed Public Enemy. Run-DMC, which included Russell's brother, "Run" Simmons, was managed by Russell and signed to Def Jam. Russell also produced the Beastie Boys' early work. It was Rubin who lost out on the next power struggle at Def Jam, leaving to form Def American Recordings, which today is American Recordings.

In 1994, with Def Jam record sales lagging, Polygram entered and bought Sony's 50 percent share, and shortly thereafter Warren G's *Regulate . . . G-Funk Era* was released, restoring the financial health of the label when it went triple platinum. LL Cool J followed with another successful album in 1995, and Foxy Brown's debut release went platinum in 1997. In 1997 Def Jam started taking note of Roc-A-Fella and its top-selling artist Jay-Z. Simmons sold his interest in Def Jam in 1998 for $100 million to Universal. Finally, in 2004, the deal that changed everything for Jay-Z, Dame Dash, and Kanye West came down the chute. Def Jam bought Roc-A-Fella in 2004 following Kanye's smash debut *The College Dropout*, and Jay-Z was appointed CEO of Def Jam; Jay-Z stayed on until the end of 2007.

NOTES

1. Associated Press Worldstream. "Kanye West Says Justin Timberlake Is His 'Biggest Inspiration and Biggest Competition.'" August 21, 2007, http://www.cbsnews.com/stories/2007/08/21/testProduction/main3188891.shtml.

2. Sean Daly. "Love Or Hate Him. Doesn't Matter." *St. Petersburg Times*, May 1, 2008.

3. Shaheem Reid. "Kanye Recovering." MTV.com, December 9, 2002.

4. Donda West. "Raising Kanye: Life Lessons from the Mother of a Hip-Hop Superstar." New York: Pocket Books, 2007.

5. Shaheem Reid. "Kanye Recovering."

6. Kimberly Davis. "Kanye West: Hip-Hop's New Big Shot." *Ebony*, April 2005.

7. Greg Kot. "Rapper's Rise: From South Side to Top of the Charts." *Chicago Tribune*, February 11, 2004.

8. Shaheem Reid. "Kanye Recovering."

9. Nui Te Koha. "Kanye's New Sort of Rap." *(Australia) Sunday Mail*, September 16, 2007.

10. Simon Vozick-Levinson. "Jay-Z's Brotherly Love." Music Q&A. *Entertainment Weekly Online*, Fall 2007.

11. Associated Press Worldstream. "Kanye West Says."

12. Nui Te Koha. "Kanye's New Sort of Rap."

13. Sway Calloway. "All Eyes on Kanye West." MTV.com, August 18, 2005.

14. Associated Press Worldstream. "Kanye West Says."

In this September 26, 2007, file photo, rapper Kanye West arrives at the Us Weekly Hot Hollywood 2007 party in Los Angeles. AP Photo/Kevork Djansezian, file.

Kanye West performs on ABC's Good Morning America concert series at New York's Lincoln Center on Friday, September 2, 2005. AP Photo/Michael Kim.

Hip-hop mogul Kanye West performs at a benefit concert at the House of Blues in Chicago on Friday, August 24, 2007. AP Photo/Brian Kersey.

Singer Kanye West tosses a towel to the crowd after performing on stage during ABC's Good Morning America summer concert series in New York's Bryant Park, in this file photo from August 4, 2006. One of the best videos for the year wasn't even nominated, according to Kanye West, the maker of said video. West, who was nominated for best pop video at the MTV Video Music Awards for "Gold Digger," says his Evil Knievel-spoof video "Touch the Sky" was better than that. AP Photo/ Paul Hawthorne-File.

Kanye West poses with his three awards at the 47th Annual Grammy Awards on Sunday, February 13, 2005, at the Staples Center in Los Angeles. West won for best rap album, best rap song, and best R&B song. AP Photo/Reed Saxon.

Kanye West poses with his award at the 2004 Billboard Music Awards Wednesday, December 8, 2004, held at the MGM Grand Garden Arena in Las Vegas. West won four awards including New Male Artist of the Year. AP Photo/Eric Jamison.

Kanye West performs at the Youth Inaugural Ball at the Washington Hilton in Washington, D.C., on Tuesday, Jan. 20, 2009. AP Photo/Carolyn Kaster.

Chapter 10

THE MUSIC

LATE REGISTRATION (2005)

When *Late Registration* was released on August 30, 2005, it had the best sales number its first week of any in Def Jam's storied hip-hop history, selling 860,000 units.

"This is me trying to become more comfortable with the position I'm in," West said. "The last album was groundbreaking. Now the process is to strive for greatness."[1]

When Kanye was working on the *Late Registration* CD, he sought out Fiona Apple's producer, Jon Brion, and decided to work with him. A fan of Apple's *When the Pawn Hits*, Kanye really liked the drum sound and the string arrangements on that album. He said he saw Brion's work as bringing Fiona's pain to real life, and he wanted that same sort of himself translated and part of *Late Registration*. Kanye said that he wanted to be the rap version of Fiona Apple.

Kanye said that the focus on sped-up soul samples was too much and that some new horizon needed to be discovered in hip-hop. The *Late Registration* album includes crescendos with horns in the background and groundbreaking drum rolls, particularly on "Diamonds from Sierra Leone," the controversy-sparking track that drew attention to the "death diamonds" coming out of Sierra Leone.

That second album was the more spiritual of Kanye's two to date at that point. The tracks "Jesus Walks," "Crack Music," and "Diamonds from Sierra Leone," Kanye says, are proof that God was speaking through Kanye with West's music.

Though the song was at first changed in name because Jay-Z had a similarly titled song, the more discussions Kanye had about diamonds, the more he learned. In fact, the diamonds became an issue West takes very serious. A well-established and respected director, Mark Romanek, who worked with Jay-Z on "99 Problems" and Q-Tip, brought up the "blood diamonds" issue, specifically how kids are killed and maimed in the West African nation.

But as West heard in the studio stories about "blood" diamonds and "conflict" diamonds, he dug deeper into it. Sierra Leone has been a major diamond exporter for more than 70 years, and in 2005 the export of diamonds alone was estimated to be at least a $250 million annual industry for the country.

The Republic of Sierra Leone is a country in West Africa with just more than 7 million people, and it is just under half the size of Kanye's birth state of Georgia. Sierra Leone is bordered by Liberia in the southeast and Guinea to the northeast, and the rest of Sierra Leone borders the Atlantic Ocean. Sierra Leone was once a high-traffic transition point for slave traders until 1787, when the capital, "Freetown," became a safe haven for freed slaves. Bordered by Liberia, which is regularly in a state of civil war, Sierra Leone had its own civil war that started in 1991 and ran through 2000, when Nigeria stepped in to restore the government and defeat rebel forces. But it is a government that ranks low, with high levels of corruption according to the United Nations, and its level of poverty is among the worst in the world. Diamonds are used to fund wars and to fill bank accounts of corrupt officials, and workers are treated mercilessly, even maimed or killed by those running the mines. Again, West was certain God was working through him to bring the issue to the forefront, to an audience that has more than a passing interest or infatuation with diamonds, to understand the dark side of the trade that needs to be exposed if it is ever going to be addressed.

West claimed the diamond industry felt like he was negatively portraying the industry. Kanye countered with the facts as he knew them: that blacks were killing each other for diamonds; the business was basically a monopoly using what could be called slave labor in certain situations.

"But how is it hurting you all for me to just tell people that there was a 10-year war in Sierra Leone where black people were killing each other over diamonds and that it was a monopoly and that there are still situations that are next to slave labor, with people working for two cups of rice a day?" West said.[2]

West, unlike a lot of artists, who are more prone to responding to the charge rather than addressing the issue, said that yes, he could be called a hypocrite for still wearing diamonds, but that he was still human and likes wearing diamonds, and rather than give them up wanted to shine light on the issue. By continuing to wear diamonds, particularly when he performs the song, he is still bringing attention to the issue. In interviews Kanye points out how the Rev. Jesse Jackson and even TV icon Bill Cosby were chastised for relationships outside of their marriages, but says that such human failings should not take away from their body of humanitarian work and that such mistakes indicate that such icons are still humans. These people are prone to the same miscues that the rest of society are— even the best stars in the brightest spotlight cast shadows, in other words. Imperfections in the messenger should not dilute or discard the entire message or body of work of such crusaders' entire lives, especially because when they can reach so many thousands and even millions in a positive way—part of being human is being a hypocrite at times, West told MTV.

Promoting the *Late Registration* album in England, Kanye demanded a London radio station play an Elton John record. He compared the album to soul singer Marvin Gaye's album *What's Going On*, released before Gaye's untimely death in 1984 (Gaye's father fatally shot him during an argument). There is a passion in Kanye's music that he said the British fans might better relate to than American fans because British fans, West said, are more appreciative of music that is not all about radio play.

The CD was also named the year's best by *Rolling Stone* magazine. West later reflected on how the second album could have been better.

"The second album, I was trying to prove something and over-rapped songs, or used too many instruments," West said. "It was like a good movie, but a long movie."[3]

Although West's lyrics are by no means sterile, comparatively they do not have the often angry or vividly violent portrayals that many rap or hip-hop albums are known for, as he explained to Britain's music publication *Timeout London*.

"A lot of hip-hop comes from the hate that hate made," West said. "People are making music to try to come out of those situations, but they still speak about what they do to get out of there. Frustrated heavy rock came out of abused white kids, and drug addicts, right? On 'Late Registration,' I have a track called 'Crack Music', which is about the music made by the crack generation. This is music that came out of the 'hood, out of the worst situations. You don't know why it's so rude, well, look where it came from."[4]

West said the whole idea that hip-hop artists are gun-toting criminals, or even violent people, is something perpetuated by the media. He points out that guns are used for entertainment in songs just like they are used in

movies, to entertain people. To sanitize rap music, to take out the reference to guns, would be akin to taking weapons out of movies:

> I think America just needs to get real when it comes to the
> way our kids speak and communicate," West told DJ Booth.
> "They need to understand what happens in rap. Tupac and
> Bigge might talk about violence, but in action movies, there are
> stunt men who actually have died on set. The amount of peo-
> ple who talk about guns, versus who actually uses them, is not
> even close in this millennium. People need to understand that
> hip-hop that has gun talk is just for entertainment; similar to if
> you were watching a movie. Film schools don't have anything
> against movies with violence. If you can approach hip-hop from
> a standpoint of, 'How did they put this together?' and get past
> the fact that they use profanity, realize that you are a reflection
> of your parents, more so then the music. Let's get more into the
> music itself. How does Dr. Dre, a musical genius, layer all these
> sounds? What about engineering and Pro Tools and the po-
> etry aspect? We can teach about hip-hop history, we can teach
> about legends, hip-hop theory. It's been around so long that text
> books can be written about it. This is a perfect time to capitalize
> on and get kids excited about (musical) education.[5]

West has since been asked if he feels that hip-hop artists are releasing songs that are about more positive things these days because of his
influence. While he says it would be politically correct to say that is the
case, he does not believe it is entirely true. He notes, though, that music
is entertainment. So it is up to the entertainers as to what they want to
rap about, just like it is up to the moviemaker what the movie is about—
inspiration and hope or crime and violence, or a combination of the two.
In fact, Kanye said he believes both the rough stuff and the positive vibes
need to be part of the art form. He admits that he is not uncomfortable
if he is a leader in what might become a move toward more positive,
spiritual, and uplifting raps. But again, he says too much of one and not
enough of the other—or one specific form above all others—would not
be the best route, either.

The second single from the album had a strong black historical tie-in to
it, from one of America's most celebrated musicians, Ray Charles. "Gold
Digger" sampled the Ray Charles song "I Got a Woman," and that part
was sung by Jamie Foxx, who played Ray Charles in the biographical fea-
ture film *Ray* about the amazing, blind entertainer. Kanye had actually

pitched the song to be used on rapper Shawnna's CD *Worth Tha Weight*, but Shawnna declined, leaving it to its owner, Kanye, who said the song was inspired after going with musical pal John Mayer to watch Foxx star as Ray Charles in the movie. The song was nominated for a Grammy Award. "Gold Digger" might not have gotten Kanye as many awards as he wanted, but at the time it set the record for most downloads in a week, 80,000, and ended up with more than one million downloads.

The third single on the album, "Heard 'Em Say," featured Adam Levine from Maroon 5, which also received critical praise.

And then came along "Touch the Sky." The song that inspired a video where West became Kanye Kanyevel, an imitation of daredevil Evel Knievel, included Pamela Anderson—former wife of Rick Salomon, Kid Rock, and Tommy Lee of Motley Crüe, and former girlfriend of Poison's Bret Michaels. The video included Nia Long, the Dallas-based Booker T. Washington High School marching band, and Tracee Ellis Ross. The video was a tribute to Knievel's failed attempt to rocket himself over the Snake River Canyon in Idaho. It unfortunately got lost in all the fiascos that resulted—a lawsuit from Knievel and award shows that did not give Kanye video of the year for this million-dollar production. Fellow Grammy-winning hip-hop artist Lupe Fiasco also sang on the song.

The most personal, and personally significant, song from the album was "Hey Mama," which was supposed to be released as a single but never was. Kanye later sang a special and emotional version of it at the 2008 Grammys (at which he won four Grammys for his follow-up album *Graduation* and also performed *Graduation*'s hit single "Stronger"). He updated the lyrics for the Grammy show to include lines about seeing his mother the night before in his dreams. Then he gave audiences on hand and watching on television one of the most sentimental Grammy speeches they had ever hear.

While Kanye pondered what he would do after *Late Registration* had run its course, given that it was part 2 in what was to become a three-part album series, he said he would feel very much like a graduate in a lot of respects once he finished with the third album. He equated the feeling to one college seniors feel when they graduate, having worked so hard to finish the degree and having completed a specific part of the journey, only to realize that they are turning a corner in their life and heading into the biggest part of all—the rest of their lives. So the fulfillment of the record, while an important achievement, left Kanye like the college senior who put in tons of hours, wrote copious amounts, sacrificed years of his life, and after having something very proud to show for it, would still be left to ask what he is supposed to do next.

GRADUATION (2007)

With *Late Registration* avoiding the traditional second-album criticism—also called the "sophomore slump"—that artists, particularly those who debut with ravenously successful debuts, often endure, West was literally ready to move on to the next part of his life, and he symbolized that with the third album's title, *Graduation*.

"This new album is simple, sweet and perfected. I think it's one of the best albums in history," West said. "In life, people are living their own movie. I wanted to make the soundtrack to that."[6]

Graduation won three Grammy awards, including best rap album. The artwork, by Japanese artist Takashi Murakami, took a long time for West to pull together, using his familiar teddy bear, though this time it appears to be in the process of being shot out of something.

The title follows the theme of the first two album titles: *The College Dropout* and *Late Registration*, which also won the Grammy for Best Rap Album, making Kanye the only hip-hop artist besides Eminem to win Grammys on his first three albums.

The album was supposed to be released in July 2007, but many delays caused Kanye to push it back to September 11, 2007, which Kanye knew was the release of 50 Cent's album, and Kanye gladly went head to head, saying "when" he outsold 50 Cent, not "if," he hoped they would still be friends because he considered 50 Cent to be not only a great artist but also intimidating.

When it comes to hip-hop music, there's nothing like a throwdown to generate interest and media attention.

When the artist 50 Cent, also known as "Fiddy," originally decided to release his new album, *Curtis*, on September 11, 2007, he figured to have the market to himself. No one was going to take on the highly successful, high-octane gangsta-rapper kingpin.

Kanye decided he wanted to go with 9/11. Someone said that this was a bad idea because it was Fiddy's release day. Kanye, not known for backing down, said that would be the release date for *Graduation* too, taking his own game to a whole new level.

50 Cent was nonplussed. He was so certain he would outsell Kanye that he made the following statement and started a battle that gained the attention of the entire music world:

"Let's raise the stakes: If Kanye West sells more records than 50 Cent on September 11, I'll no longer write music," 50 Cent said. "I'll write music and work with my other artists, but I won't put out anymore solo albums."[7]

The first sales figures would have led to Fiddy's early retirement, because *Graduation* commenced with 957,000 in sales out of the gate, compared to 691,000 for 50 Cent.

There's more than four bits of value to 50 Cent. In a lot of ways, he is the epitome of old-school rap and new-school business savvy.

Since the killings of Tupac—or 2-Pac—and Biggie Smalls, few epitomize hip-hop and rap's hard-edge image better than Curtis James Jackson III, also known as 50 Cent (or Fiddy, or Fitty, depending on the publication). He was born in 1975 in South Jamaica, which is in New York City's borough of Queens. His mother Sabrina, a cocaine dealer at the time, was 15 when she gave birth to her son, and the baby's father was nowhere to be found. Sabrina raised Curtis alone until he was eight, when she was drugged unconscious and left in her apartment with the gas turned on and windows shut, killing her. Curtis moved in with his grandparents and a total of eight aunts and uncles, and his grandmother simply told Curtis, "You are going to stay with us now. Your mother's not coming home."[8]

Curtis started boxing at age 11 and actually competed in a meet that was a precursor to the Junior Olympics. But Curtis started dealing crack cocaine at age 12 in 1987, capitalizing on the crack epidemic that was sweeping the country. He told his grandparents he was involved in several after-school activities to cover for what he was doing as he built his reputation as a crack-cocaine dealer. As a sophomore at Andrew Jackson High School, he was busted passing through a metal detector with a gun and drugs on him. He claims he was too honest to lie to his grandmother anymore, so he simply told her he was a drug dealer, and that was that.[9]

But his business hit a snag in 1994 when a new customer turned out to be an undercover police officer. Less than a month later, police executed a search warrant on his house and found cocaine, a gun, and heroin. Facing as many as nine years in prison, Fiddy opted for a "boot camp" program, where young offenders—he had just turned 19—are put through a rigorous army-like orientation requiring discipline, respect, and physical fitness training. He earned his GED and served just six months. Once out of the program, he became "50 Cent," a name he borrowed from infamous 1980s Brooklyn bandit Kelvin Martin. But Curtis said he took the moniker to indicate a literal "change" and noted that he was proud to be like Clark in that he too would do whatever it took to provide for himself.[10]

He went from boot camp to another kind of highly specialized, often intense training, joining with one of hip-hop's founding fathers in terms of commercial success, Jam Master Jay of Run-DMC. Jay was starting his own label and taught 50 Cent in 1996 how to count bars, write songs, and make records. He "unofficially" released an album in 2000, *The Power of the Dollar,* for which he recorded 36 songs; only 18 were included

But he made a bigger mark by releasing a stand-alone single, "How to Rob," which describes how he would rob artists. Jay-Z was among a group of artists who responded the way rap artists do, by slamming 50 Cent onstage in a song. However, the hip-hop artist Nas liked the song and the controversy it generated—gangsta rap and street cred were the building blocks of a successful rapper at that point—so he invited 50 Cent to tour with him. However, on May 24, 2000, just before 50 Cent was to do a video and thus finally have an official album and career set to take off, he visited his grandmother's apartment in South Jamaica, Queens. Fiddy's young son was in the house. Fiddy started to leave and returned to get some jewelry. When he got back in the car, in the back seat, another car pulled up, and a gunman holding a 9 millimeter automatic blew nine rounds into 50 Cent, hitting him in the hand, arm, hip, legs, chest, and face. After two weeks in the hospital, 50 Cent, with a slur in his voice, a wisdom tooth blown out from one of the nine bullets, and another wound in his right hand where the bullet hit his thumb and exited his pinky, was released. The gunman, Darryl "Hommo" Baum, was a former bodyguard of heavyweight champion Mike Tyson, something a young 50 Cent was very aware of from his own interest in boxing. A week after 50 Cent was out of the hospital, Baum was killed, gunned down. Mike Tyson then offered a $50,000 "hit" on the two gang members who were suspected of killing Baum.[11]

The shooting gave 50 Cent some time to reflect. He healed in Pennsylvania's Poconos with his son and his girlfriend at the time. Confined to using a walker to get around for the first six weeks after the shooting, 50 Cent attacked the gym with ferocity over the next five months and built the muscular physique that he carries to this day.

He also had his rap career back on track—or so it appeared—while recovering, signing a music publishing deal with Columbia Records. However, after word got out that he had been shot, the contract was pulled, and 50 Cent was blackballed within the music industry. He finally went to Canada just to record in the studio and basically start over again, from scratch. So many times he had been to the cusp of stardom—the first record deal, the album that was never officially released, the boost that touring with Nas would have given him, and the publishing deal with well-respected Columbia—only to disappear from the music scene's radar.

Finally, the tracks in Canada were enough for an album, but he had to release it on his own, independently, meaning it would not be distributed in stores or even get radio airplay for the most part. But someone did hear the tracks on *Guess Who's Back,* a young superstar named Marshall Mathers.

Fiddy was actually discovered by Eminem, the most well-known—and within the industry itself, most accepted and respected—white rapper, though that list includes really only Eminem and Vanilla Ice, the latter of whom was bounced out of the industry after a one-bit hit and a gimmick image. Fiddy worked with Eminem and rap legend Dr. Dre at the then-infamous label Interscope after putting out his own debut album in 2002. In a strange way, 50 Cent represented everything Eminem himself wanted to portray: toughness and street savvy. Though Eminem had survived the "white projects" of Detroit and had his own rough upbringing, he did not have the violent gangsta credentials that 50 Cent wore tattooed in his skin as bullet holes. And Eminem had what 50 Cent wanted musically; Eminem was a well-respected artist who few had believed in at one time but who had believed so deeply in himself that, by sheer will, he had carved out an opportunity and then pushed himself atop the rap world where a lot of people, especially early on, believed he had no place, culturally or musically.

His record deal with Dr. Dre paid 50 Cent a cool $1 million, and his first album, *Get Rich or Die Tryin'* in 2003, was quite autobiographical and accurate—and successful, moving 872,000 units in the first four days of release and debuting at number 1 on the Billboard 100. *Massacre,* released in 2005, was an even bigger success, selling 1.14 million copies the first four days. With Tupac and Biggie victims of violent shooting deaths, hip-hop had its new platinum thug.

But 50 Cent had become a savvy businessman in a short amount of time, even exceeding his mentor Eminem's own entrepreneurial efforts. Like Jay-Z, 50 Cent had been given good advice to create his own brand and get involved in as many successful business ventures loosely tied to his musical career as he could. He started his own G-Unit clothing line and as part of it inked a five-year deal in 2003 with Reebok for his own shoe line to be distributed. His more successful venture, though, was the deal he collaborated on with Glaceau, to create Formula 50, a vitamin water drink playing on his name. Though the drink was a success, 50 Cent really cashed in when Coca-Cola (it could be called Fiddy's biggest Coke deal ever) bought Glaceau. Because part of 50 Cent's deal with Glaceau gave him a share of the company, he was reported to, after taxes, have taken home $100 million from Coke's purchase. Keeping his image as the gangsta rapper, he has also lent his name, likeness, and voice to a series of violent video games. In addition, he branched off into acting, starring, like Eminem, in a semiautobiographical account of his own life with Terrance

Howard, *Get Rich or Die Tryin*, but also had a role in the 2006 Iraq war movie *Home of the Brave*, playing a soldier who comes home traumatized after killing an Iraqi woman.

At the top of his game, 50 Cent decided that Kanye West had a lot of nerve picking the same release date for his next album, September 11, 2007. West was pulling in fans from all over the map, while 50 Cent was hoping his music and reputation would carry the day.

Game On

Black Entertainment Television (BET) had both performers on for *Top 10 Live*. By winning a coin toss, 50 Cent was allowed to open the show and rapped his top single, "Ayo Technology," and in the interview that followed declared that West did not stand a chance to beat him in the album sales battle. Fiddy went so far to say things were going so well, and were going to improve so much, that he was considering even releasing another album that year, something he would surely not do if he wasn't confident that he could drub West. Fiddy did say it was just a competitive situation, that he did not harbor any resentment toward West popping his release date, but added at first he did not think West's choice of release date was a good idea.

If one were to base a guess on how the album sales would go on that night's performance, Kanye came out with all his cards face up—and an ace up his sleeve by bringing Jay-Z to perform "Big Brother" with him from *Graduation*.

During an interview afterward that included both Fiddy and Kanye, Fiddy started to waver, claiming if Kanye won, it was because Fiddy was the defending champ, and people were tired of seeing him win all the time. West broke it down to basics, saying his new album was set to be the best of what music represented at that particular time and that he wouldn't put the Kanye West stamp on it if it wasn't the highest possible quality.

Kanye said there was more being done to fan the flames of rivalry in the media than meets the casual eye. Indeed, he said the press loves making gray areas into black-and-white opinions, but likes even more pitting black against black.

"The amount of press we got was real. Everything was real. You're dealing with real people in that environment," Kanye said. "The press wanted to make it a beef because that's what they want. They want the black guys to be up against each other, about to shoot each other. And that's not what they got. What they got is two black guys selling a lot of records."[12]

Game Over

Although West dusted the floor with him in the battle of their 2007 releases, 50 Cent can claim some solace in the fact that he did debut at number 1 on the Swiss and Irish charts, though Kanye owned the biggest markets, including the United States, Britain and Canada.

Although *Graduation* had only a couple of singles that rocketed up the charts, the album was praised by critics for top–to-bottom being his most solid yet, and critics praised him at length for improving as a lyricist. *Rolling Stone* noted that the songs on the album "improve on every listen: This is an album that you first like, then love." The *Chicago Tribune* reviewed it as West "at his best." Jay-Z, an executive at Kanye's label, and who has both had his own work produced by Kanye and contributed to Kanye's tracks, said every song on *Graduation* is good, and that's because of how much time and effort West puts into each and every track.

"It's pretty much how much he cares about it; it not done for any other reason but to be the best music out at that specific time," Jay-Z told *Entertainment Weekly*.

> You know, at times you could hear [other] people's music, and you hear, "Okay, that's your girl single, that's the thug single, that's the . . . " No, it's none of that. Every single song he makes, he makes because he thinks it's the best record at that specific time. He may not think it next week, but that week, he thought that was the best record that he could make. We have 75 mixes of "Stronger." Who does that? When I was sitting in mastering to make sure the album got done, he was somewhere in Sweden sending through mixes of "Good Life"—16 different mixes of the song, who does that?

Kanye's guest list on *Graduation* is a list of music royalty. The track "Good Morning" is sampled from the Elton John classic "Someone Save My Life Tonight," and "Champion" comes from the legendary band Steely Dan, which agreed to let Kanye used it only after he called them personally and told them how he wanted it to be a sort of message to his father, whose relationship he has off and on struggled with through the years.

Yet the biggest hit on the album, the breathtaking and inspirational "Stronger," is simply a Kanye-esque amped-up, full-of-passion sample of Daft Punk's "Harder, Better, Faster, Stronger."

The hit "I Wonder" digs deep into the rich well of hip-hop, sampling the song Tupac performed, "Ambition Az A Ridah." Kanye went to his longtime inspiration Michael Jackson and his hit "Pretty Young Thing" for the track "Good Life." Other tracks include elements from Public Enemy, Common, and the classic group Chairmen of the Board.

The album made the top 10 worldwide with three exceptions: it went no higher than 16 in Finland and 13 in Japan and fared its worst in Italy, where it never moved past number 33 on the Italian charts.

"Stronger" seems to be a song that will live long into the future, and it has such appeal that it could link up as a possible endorsement deal for anything from a sporting goods manufacturer to a sports drink. The other songs are the kind that are widely regarded as simply being good music, and the CD, from start to finish, seemed like one it was easier to spend the extra money to buy in whole rather than download so many good songs one by one.

Another inspirational song, or at least one for reflection, is "I Wonder," something West knows is a thought that goes through a lot of graduates' minds when they leave school.

"I have a song called 'I Wonder'—it talks about that, like what do you do in your life, like where are you headed, how do you make these decisions," West said. "I offer a little—a little—advice, but more just posing that question and letting them zone out to the music and figure it out themselves."[13]

No one was happier for Kanye West in the hip-hop world than Jay-Z, West's mentor and record label exec. Jay-Z had seen Kanye come in as a producer eager to break into the craft, and now he was able to see West atop once again as an artist, achieving even bigger numbers than the already remarkable sales Kanye's first two albums had achieved. West's debut album, *The College Dropout,*" did 440,000 units its first week, and *Late Registration* did very nearly double that, with 860,000 copies. Doing 100,000 more copies than that with *Graduation* was just icing on an already stratospheric-reaching cake. As an artist, producer, and music executive, Jay-Z said Kanye's battle mano-a-mano with 50 Cent was the case of a rising tide lifting both ships, and he is certain that neither Kanye nor 50 Cent would have posted such big numbers either had the battle not garnered so much free publicity in the media.

It also came at just the right time, as rap CD sales were dropping at a rate that threatened the industry's ability to move forward into the future. But Jay-Z is no neophyte, and he knew that magical first week was due to a special occurrence between an established old-school heavyweight and rap's biggest rising star and that only such a confluence of events and circumstance led to more than 1.5 million combined units selling. However, it was also a wake-up call to the industry and artists that with the right amount of hard work and creative marketing, big numbers could be done, and certain CDs could be launched as significant events—those days are by no means over. Jay-Z said that he certainly does not want to see 50 Cent go away and that having that kind of competition boosted his own artist, Kanye.

Jay-Z was in and around Kanye as the latter put together the CD and remembers West sometimes turning in a dozen, or even dozens, of remix versions of particular tracks. While critics praised West's album, Jay-Z had several favorite tracks. And though he was not featured on Kanye's CD this time around—though he had been slated to be on at least one song—the hit "Big Brother" was written by Kanye and about his special relationship with Jay-Z. More than just his personal connection to that song, Jay-Z said he think it is Kanye's best work since "Jesus Walks."

Though "Big Brother" sounds like a tribute song—and it is—it is also critical at times of the pair's relationship. But that's the kind of artistic integrity Jay-Z expects and admires from West.

True to his goal of bettering and sustaining hip-hop, the week after the first sales figures were announced, 50 Cent released a remix of "I Get Money" with a verse from Jay-Z. Although Jay-Z would not let that track drop with the CD to be in direction competition with the first week's sales war, it was a gesture that showed West remained a supporter of other rap artists and would still make time for a hard-core, old-school rapper like 50 Cent even though he is the competition.

Kanye told ABC News's *Nightline* that *Graduation* is a CD that appeals to listeners across genres.

"This, this CD is for everyone," Kanye said. "I don't please everybody with who I am as a person. I'm just trying to please myself with who I am as a person. But I make a product. And I am the Coca-Cola, the Walt Disney, the, who else can we say just has full rein?"[14]

Graduation also further developed the Kanye West brand, and West said it showed the commitment to quality was ever-constant and even improving.

"A lot of hip-hop artists don't have the ability to make classic songs because they spend most of their time rapping about themselves rather than what people care about," West said. "My songs are songs. They are songs to help in life, to inspire. Let me speak in the third person for a second—a Kanye West album is like a brand, like Louis Vuitton, or Nike, or the latest Jordans. You buy a pair of Jordans, take them to school and everybody goes 'Wow'. Second pair, 'Incredible.' Third pair, you don't even have to say it. It's like me. People just know. It's a Kanye West."[15]

WEST AS "OWNER" STRUGGLES

On GOOD's Web site, SonyBMG proudly brags about how after he was pursued by virtually every music company, their company signed Kanye West to develop his own recording label, an effort that would see West recruit and develop talent. The second paragraph, almost invisible in small type, notes, "Such deals, which can be extremely expensive and often fail, have become rarer."[16]

If Kanye West's career as a label owner was a song, a lot of people would be curious to hear the ending. Kanye started directing his own label when Sony brought him on board—not as an artist, but rather as a label owner. This is not an illogical step for top-selling artists, especially those who have also experienced a lot of success as a producer, as Kanye has.

GOOD is Kanye's label with Sony, and it stands for Getting Out Our Dreams. He signed Grammy winner John Legend, Chicago rap legend Common, Consequence, GLC, Fonzworth Bentley, Sa-Ra, gangsta I. Crisis, and others.

Only John Legend, however, has been an indisputable success, with about 3.5 million combined sales of his two GOOD releases and three Grammy nominations for 2004's *Get Lifted*.

Common, still trying to find his market after the critically acclaimed *Resurrection* years ago (which did not do well commercially), sold 800,000 copies of 2005's *Be* and dropped to about 500,000 copies for 2007's *Finding Forever*. Common is a close friend to Kanye, and they are linked by both a deep friendship and their connection to Chicago. The pair was brought together by Chicago rap icon No I.D. when Kanye was a teenager. Common's career has not been without constant distractions, many of them brought on by himself, though others seem to have been a matter of circumstance. Whether Common, who was initially known as Common Sense, wanted to involve himself in the East Coast–West Coast rap wars, was simply trying to sell records, or simply ticked off the wrong people by accident, Common's "I Used to Love Her" song from *Resurrection* took some jabs at the direction hip-hop was heading with the California-based violent gangsta rap. Never one to ignore—and loving to ignite—a beef, Westside Connection flamed Common's song title with profanities. After *Resurrection* got more attention, a Los Angeles reggae band with the name Common Sense sued Common, who was forced to remove "Sense" and go by just Common. Finally, Westside Connection and Common sat down with controversial Louis Farrakhan and agreed to stop going after each other. Common has also been, since childhood, a member of Chicago's Trinity United Church of Christ, which of course was led by Rev. Jeremiah Wright, who was thrust as an issue into the 2008 U.S. presidential campaign as Democrat Barack Obama's church and pastor—Wright also attended Virginia Union University, a decade before Donda West went to that same university to get her undergraduate degree.

But Kanye's production magic has not helped Common develop that magical album that will send him into the top echelon of hip-hop artists. Common continues to try to find his style, and West has worked tirelessly to help Common reach that goal. For whatever reason, Common still cannot break down that "million in sales" number or have that signature hit that he has been seeking for so long now. Common did receive four Grammy nominations for the West-produced *Be* album.

Consequence, thought to be a rising star in hip-hop, has fared even worse on GOOD, with his 2007 *Don't Quit Your Day Job* selling just 140,000 copies.

West now calls running his own label one of the biggest mistakes he has ever made in life, and he has gone to the seemingly odd extreme of blaming it on Sony, claiming that the company offered him the label and that he had never asked for it.

The GOOD Web site refers to him as "KanYe" West, as West often goes by "Ye," and claims the limit is endless for the self-proclaimed best-dressed label in music.

And although it has had its artists win several awards and receive nominations for more, the future looks pretty bleak for GOOD music. West is running into something he never saw in his path—limits. He noted he did not have the time to push for more radio play for his GOOD artists when he was trying to get airtime for *Graduation*, his 2007 release with the label he still records for, Def Jam's Roc-A-Fella.

The man who wanted to make the final decision on everything was exhausted when his phone would ring, and someone would want him to sign off on specifications for a new song or even clothes for a video shoot.

So the future for the label is cloudy, at best, and West finds himself with a stable of artists, many of whom do not feel like their albums and singles are getting the kind of support and marketing push their music deserves.

Kanye's greatest strengths in some cases are proving to be his greatest liabilities. He is a control freak and admits to being so obsessive-compulsive that he will make a dozen or more remixes of a single song. He cannot let go until he exhausts every option he sees. That exhausts those around him, and it also exhausts a considerable amount of both his time and his energy.

He decided to remodel the house he bought in Los Angeles, and after it took longer than expected, he had it ripped apart and started again because he did not like how it turned out.

His fashion line Pastelle was plagued by constant delays because Kanye had to learn about fabrics and other parts of the industry that need to be understood by designers, not just what goes good with what or which primary colors work with others.

He signed with Louis Vuitton—which seemed appropriate, given that Kanye has often been called in the media the "Louis Vuitton Don"—in a long-awaited agreement to design for the high-end fashion company.

Kanye announced in May 2008 that his West Brands, LLC, had launched Kanye Travel Ventures, which involved working with a travel consultancy to develop high-quality and cost-effective travel experiences for Kanye fans. The press release includes quotes from consultant Neil Abrams, who will run the operational part of this Kanye venture, asserting that "while celebrity brand-driven travel programs have been attempted in the past, none have demonstrated long-term viability." And Kanye West, hip-hop superstar, has a successful travel business record on to base such a launch?

Ray West, Kanye's father, opened a store to sell water in Maryland and, to promote the store, had Kanye come to town to lead a walk for "World Water Day."[17] How many people turned out to see in 2007 the most well-known, award-winning, leading artist and walk with him and talk about water? Maybe 100,000? Perhaps 10,000? The *Washington Post* reported 50 people came out for the walk, several of whom admitted to being fans. Kanye, who backed his father's venture financially, liked the idea of clean, good water for Maryland and was proud to support his father's undying entrepreneurial spirit. As of August 2008, the number for Ray West's water store is out of order, and e-mails to the Web site promoting it were not answered.

If Kanye had nothing else going on in 2007, this still would have been a taxing proposal—producing for Roc-A-Fella, running his own label, and launching his travel business and his father's water business—but he also had his own album. And with everything on the line going head-to-head with 50 Cent, he had to promote his own album first and foremost. He was also doing book signings with his mother through summer 2007 to promote her largely biographical book that included a few stories about what Kanye's childhood was like. Kanye had videos for his albums to make, remixes to produce, and the ever-growing contingent of collaborators he contributed his voice to, in addition to getting ideas for his next album.

Kanye's management team in 2008 was excited about Kanye resigning with Pepsi, and even a "multiplatform" sort of branding deal with its chief competitor, Coke. Although multiplatform is a key branding term and is important to keep in mind because artists and endorsers need to be promoted strategically across such mediums as print, TV, radio, and the Internet, it is hard to imagine Pepsi or Coke wanting to share an artist's creative energy, even if it is not in product overlap.

Kanye is in the position he always wanted to be in—the opportunities are limitless, his phone rings nonstop, and the e-mail inbox is constantly overflowing. The young man who had to jump up on executives' desks to get their attention and beg for someone to listen finds himself in a position now where everyone wants to listen, everyone wants to give him an audience—but no one has the guts to tell the powerful icon it might be time to close his mouth or to limit the spreading of his name, image, endorsements, and time. Certainly, he has surrounded himself with a management team, and that team sifts through the slew of endorsement opportunities, and Kanye does have to approve them all, but at some point, enough will be more than enough—it will be too much.

Two of his recent ventures, the GOOD recording label[18] and the travel venture,[19] include notes in their press release about how such versions are quite unlikely to succeed. Without a business background or education, Kanye is in a position many artists, entertainers, and athletes find themselves in, where people are banging at the door hoping to cash in on their name. Even the water-store business with his father was fraught with risk and very little upside, though attaching the business to the cause of good water for everyone worldwide was certainly a good marketing move.

Only opportunities that make good branding and common sense, such as the Louis Vuitton venture because of Kanye's relative fashion expertise and interest, are worth West's time and energy. Cashing in merely for the check will damage his image in the long run. Certainly, having his tour sponsored by Pepsi or him simply endorsing such a well-regarded brand makes good business sense and provides Kanye with a good payday for relatively little of his time, and music talents such as Michael Jackson and Britney Spears have had successful endorsement runs with Pepsi, but they also have made bad personal decisions and destroyed their image at times. He could even cross-brand by marketing his videos with Pepsi commercials, like country star Toby Keith did to launch his album via an endorsement deal once his label had lost interest in him.

What his advisers might end up telling Kanye—or what he might see from the public—is that he has to keep his top priority his own musical career because if that suffers, so will his brand, and the opportunities that come his way will be limited in both quantity and quality if that is the case.

NOTES

1. Chris Norris. "Top of the World." *Blender*, September 2005.

2. Sway Calloway. "All Eyes on Kanye West." MTV.com, August 18, 2005.

3. Nui Te Koha. "Kanye's New Sort of Rap." *(Australia) Sunday Mail*, September 16, 2007.

4. Alex Raymer. "Kanye West: Interview." *Timeout London*, September 14, 2005.

5. DJ Booth. "Kanye West Interview." DJBooth.net, September 3, 2007.

6. Nui Te Koha. "Kanye's New Sort of Rap."

7. BBC News. "50 Cent Will Quit if Sales Fail." August 11, 2007.

8. Lola Ogunnaike. "50 Cent: Taking Care of Business." *Rolling Stone*, September 20, 2007.

9. Shaheem Reid. "50 Cent: Money to Burn." http://www.mtv.com/bands/123/50_Cent/news_feature_021203/index.jhtml.

10. Tone Boots. "Get Rich or Die Trying: Meet the Original 50 Cent—The Gangster who Inspired the Biggest Name in Rap." *Stuff*, August 3, 2005, http://stuff.maxim.com/articles/index.aspx?id=1112.

11. Stephanie Cohen. "Tyson In Hit Bid." *New York Post*, June 13, 2008, http://www.nypost.com/seven/06132008/news/regionalnews/tyson_in_hit_bid_witness_115319.htm.

12. Terry Moran. "Home with Kanye West." *Nightline*, ABC News, September 24, 2007.

13. *Popworld*. "Kanye West Interview." Channel 4, Great Britain, July 8, 2007.

14. Terry Moran. "Home with Kanye West."

15. Nui Te Koha. "Kanye's New Sort of Rap."

16. GOOD Music Label. Official Web site. http://www.GettingOutOur Dreams.com.

17. Mike James. "Business Runs on Water." BlackEnterprise.com, March 7, 2007.

18. GOOD Music Label. Official Web site. http://www.GettingOutOurDreams.com.

19. Neil Abrams. "Kanye West Launches New Online Travel Program." PR Newswire, March 31, 2008.

Chapter 11

HURRICANE KATRINA MEETS HURRICANE KANYE

NBC hosted a fundraiser for Hurricane Katrina victims. The well-intentioned show was typical of a cause-based program, with celebrities reading thoughtful, though scripted, text about the plight of the victims of the hurricane.

About the same time, the Bush administration was still reeling from its lack of timely response to the hurricane, the disjointed operation to provide relief, and an overall perception that the government either did not take forecasters' advice seriously or simply was unprepared for the disaster.

During the program, former *Saturday Night Live* star Mike Myers, a comedian from Canada who also starred in the Austin Powers and Wayne's World movies, was featured on the NBC relief effort with Kanye West.

After Myers read from the script, Kanye looked uncomfortable as he stared at the teleprompter. And being true to himself, he came up with words of his own, forsaking the script and igniting a national controversy. West was following the news coverage of the hurricane more closely than others. He had noticed how blacks were being accused of stealing from stores they entered, whereas whites were frequently said to be getting supplies.

"I hate the way they portray us in the media. You see a black family, it says, 'They're looting,'" West said on NBC passionately as Myers looked on, caught off-guard. "You see a white family, it says, 'They're looking for food.' And, you know, it's been five days [waiting for relief supplies] because most of the people are black. And even for me to complain about it, I would be a hypocrite because I've tried to turn away from the TV, because it's too hard to watch."

West took part of the blame himself, claiming he should have reached sooner and dug deeper in his pocket to provide relief and a good thought to those struggling from the disaster.

"I've even been shopping before even giving a donation, so now I'm calling my business manager right now to see what is the biggest amount I can give, and just to imagine if I was down there, and those are my people down there," West said. "So anybody out there that wants to do anything that we can help—with the way America is set up to help the poor, the black people, the less well-off, as slow as possible. I mean, the Red Cross is doing everything they can. We already realize a lot of people that could help are at war right now, fighting another way—and they've given them permission to go down and shoot us."

Myers looked toward the camera and studied West again. West finished speaking, and Myers was cued and began reading from the teleprompter.

"And subtle, but in many ways even more profoundly devastating, is the lasting damage to the survivors' will to rebuild and remain in the area," Myers said on NBC's Hurricane Katrina fundraiser. "The destruction of the spirit of the people of southern Louisiana and Mississippi may end up being the most tragic loss of all."

At that point, Kanye could hardly contain himself. He was fed up with the grim picture and the media portrayal that whites were taking food needed for survival, while blacks were doing nothing but stealing big-screen televisions.

"George Bush doesn't care about black people," West said into the camera to a nationwide audience.

NBC issued a statement after the show, claiming it did not want the focus to be on West's criticism of the president—even though West was the one celebrity to express an honest feeling rather than read from a script—and wanted it to be on the money donated for the just cause.

"Tonight's telecast was a live television event wrought with emotion," parent company NBC Universal said in a statement issued to reporters after the broadcast. "Kanye West departed from the scripted comments that were prepared for him, and his opinions in no way represent the views of the networks. It would be most unfortunate if the efforts of the artists who participated tonight and the generosity of millions of Americans who are helping those in need are overshadowed by one person's opinion."

After being so caught off-guard by West's candidness on the NBC show, Myers later told Moviefone that Kanye's point was well taken.

"I went to the Katrina telethon because I was very moved by the plight of the people in New Orleans, and I wanted to make a difference," said Myers, who also gave West a cameo in the 2008 movie *Love Guru*. "I think that the frustration that Kanye expressed was valid."[1]

West, as usual, did not have any regrets, as he explained later. He said he left the fundraiser on NBC with a clear conscience, and if nothing else, he was true to himself and expressed his honest feelings that night with Myers.

"I think it changed my life for the better," West said of criticizing President Bush. "I think people understood me a little bit more. And instead of this guy like, has little baby Tourette's maybe not quite diagnosed—but the truth just comes out, like accidentally, like what's on the top of his mind. I'm working off the cusp here, I'm working off the top of my mind, I'm not reading the teleprompter, I'm speaking from the heart, and that thing got dialed up and typed into the heart, and that was that. I mean, I have a hard time believing that George Bush cares about anyone, so sidebar, black people also."[2]

West said being honest is the most important thing, and he has no qualms with people disagreeing with his opinion on the now-former president.

"I said what I said emotionally," West told a South Australia newspaper. "I dealt with the praise and I dealt with the backlash. It is what it is. My main goal is to let people know I'm a musician, not a politician. I don't know anything about politics. I care about people."[3]

Kanye's mother Donda, in an interview with the *Baltimore Sun*, said her son's comments about President Bush were from Kanye's heart, and whether anyone agreed with him or not, they should respect Kanye being honest about his opinion, and if nothing else, the comment opened a public dialogue about opinions people had privately about both the hurricane response and the perception that blacks, and not whites, were looting, and whites were simply getting supplies to survive.

"In my view, there is to be some consideration for what is politically correct, but there is to be more consideration for telling the truth and making the most positive impact on society that we can," Donda said. "Kanye is really, I think, a very good spokesperson. He's a very critical and analytical thinker, as he was taught to be . . . If you think that what is happening is very unjust, and you have the platform like Kanye to call attention to it, I think it's very responsible of him to do that, and it's the responsibility of the person listening to decide if they agree."[4]

Months later, Kanye had no regrets.

"I knew I wasn't going to read the whole script, because we'd practiced that earlier," West said. "I didn't think about Bush until the telethon. I saw him [on the TV]. I'm like, 'Wait a second, dude, that guy over there, he doesn't care,'" West said in a *Rolling Stone* interview. "But America was already headed that way. I think it was a common opinion."[5]

AWARDS SHOW FLAPS

In 2004 Kanye walked out of the American Music Awards, saying he felt like he was robbed at the November 15 show after not winning Best New Artist.

The artist Kanye lost to, country music sensation Gretchen Wilson, had become the media darling of country music, and her timing could not have been better. A self-proclaimed "red-neck woman," also the name of her first song, which went to number 1, Wilson is a former bartender from Pocahontas, Illinois, a rural outpost in the Midwest. She was born to a 16-year-old mother and was raised by her mother after he father left when Gretchen was just two years old, forcing Gretchen and her mom to live in poverty in trailer parks. Gretchen dropped out of high school as a freshman to get a job as a cook, though she eventually finished her GED in 2007 at age 34.

That America was in the grips of arguably its most-ever conservative period lent itself to a "redneck" becoming a musical force in the industry. Wilson was an unapologetically hard partier—her second hit was "Here for the Party"—and lived in the backwoods, road ATVs, and drank a lot of whiskey, even while on her tour bus being filmed by CMT, the country equivalent of MTV. It was a rags-to-riches story that even *60 Minutes* devoted a full segment to, hearing about how Wilson would both break up and start fights in the rural bar she tended in. Wilson came along when country artists, particularly women, had been crossing over considerably into pop mainstream, with artists such as Shania Twain and Faith Hill blending the line between country and pop. Country was hungry for a return to its roots, as were a lot of the more traditional, rough-edged female singers who lived lives much like the depressing country songs, such as Lorrie Morgan, Tammy Wynette, and Loretta Lynn. Wilson was a return to those less glamorous, more edgy roots, and with a gravelly voice, she was Nashville's pride and joy. However, since her next release, *All Jacked Up*, which included the radio single "Homewrecker," Wilson has been as quiet as her hometown of Pocahontas, though she released a new album in 2008. After a failed marriage to a former bandmate, Gretchen had a child, Grace, with her boyfriend, though they split up shortly after the release of her second CD.

Kanye, who was reportedly more sad than angry backstage at the 2004 AMAs, said he did take satisfaction out of the fact that one of his CD's biggest hits, "Jesus Walks," was still getting good airplay. Kanye had been nominated for three American Music Awards, and was shut out.

On November 3, 2006, at the MTV Europe Music Awards in Copenhagen, Denmark, Kanye West crashed the stage when the award for best video was being presented to Justice and Simian for "We Are Your Friends." West said that by not picking him, the show lost credibility. The video West was so proud of was "Touch the Sky," an elaborate, million-dollar production featuring Pamela Anderson and Kanye as a modern-day Evel Knievel. Kanye had been honored earlier in the show with the Best Hip-Hop Artist award. But when he crashed the stage, he told the world that if he did not win, the show lost credibility. The clip appeared not only live on MTV, but also around the world on cable, in print publications, and online.

However, West followed up this flap by apologizing while on tour with U2 in Australia and also spoofed himself on the NBC late-night show *Saturday Night Live*, which included Kanye interrupting the Nobel Prize. Critics applauded the self-deprecating move, and that he was willing to play a part in poking fun at himself told people that somewhere, under all the bragging, was a sense of humor and an honest sense of humility.

West later said he was joking around at the European event and that the way it turned into such a big deal was ridiculous. He also said he is trying not to freak out as frequently because he does not want to come off as a jerk.

At the 2007 MTV Video Music Awards in Las Vegas, West had five nominations and did not win a single award. Worse to Kanye, he had to perform from a suite in the Palms Hotel rather than in the show's theater. Because his friend—and the person whom West considered his greatest competition for awards—Justin Timberlake got to perform both in a suite and on the theater stage to end the show, West felt cheated and said so, further deepening his rift with the music network.

After the dust had settled following the VMAs, Kanye was giving an interview to a major U.S. magazine at a party in Los Angeles when a camera crew approached to catch the interview on tape. But it turned out the crew was from MTV, whom West had yet to forgive. West put his hand over the camera, told the crew and sound workers he had no problem with them, just their bosses at MTV, and did not take his hand off the camera lens until his interview with the magazine writer was complete.

Days later, Kanye told his entire side of the MTV flap.

"Let me do the politically correct disclaimer and say that MTV has done a lot for me through the years," West said, documenting step by step how he felt MTV has passed him over several times for awards he deserved, including recognition for "Gold Digger" and "Touch the Sky."[6]

Kanye also took time on the *Ellen DeGeneres Show* to speak out on the controversial performance to open the MTV VMAs by Britney Spears, who did not perform well and was ridiculed publicly and in the media for what was considered by all to be a very poor performance, something West felt everyone could have seen during rehearsal—and should have prevented.

> "I just felt like she wasn't ready and I felt like you know, they had to get their ratings," West said. "At the end of the day, they did what they had to do. It shows you it's not a black-and-white thing; it's a money thing. Someone had to be at that practice and be like, 'Wow, this is not good,' like all the lip-syncing and everything. I mean, that performance, if had it been pulled off perfectly, still wouldn't have been up to par to start off the MTV Awards. Cause I'm a fan of these award shows. I told these guys at MTV, I said look there are only a couple of things important in music this year, 'Umbrella,' Amy Winehouse— it's not just me. Britney Spears is not important to music right now. She's important to the tabloids and stuff like that. I felt bad for her, bad for everyone involved."[7]

West did later apologize for his outburst after the MTV Awards show that was caught on tape and broadcast on YouTube.

"I'm trying hard, man. I got the number one record, man. I was wrong for, you know, spazzing out, you know?" Kanye said. "And people would ask me about it, you know, the days afterwards. And I would just keep on talking about things they did wrong, which is just a justification. But, you know, as a man, I need to own up to what I do and I can't justify."[8]

TAKING A STAND

When Kanye was three years old, his parents divorced, and his mother moved him with her to Chicago. He would visit his father on spring break, during the summer, and over Christmas holidays each year. He had been extremely close to his father, calling him his everything, but the divorce brought him and his mother closer together than they had ever been.

That worried Kanye—that people would call him a mama's boy, if only because of the living situation.

West honestly admits that not having a father figure around him during those years shaped him significantly. He logically points out that spending more time around his mother, he modeled himself more after her than his father, simply because he was around her more. He said that people would pick up on the fact that he acted more like his mother and that kids at school would accuse him of "acting like a [homosexual]" and ask him, "Dog, are you gay?" throughout his high school years. The result was that Kanye became overly macho when it came to sexuality.

"And what happened was it made me kind of homophobic, 'cause I would go back and question myself," Kanye said. "If you see something and you don't want to be that because there's such a negative connotation toward it, you try to separate yourself from it so much that it made me homophobic by the time I was through high school. Anybody that was gay I was like, 'Yo, get away from me.'"[9]

West started hanging out with friends who he said looked like thugs, and that is where he felt he found his manhood and male role models. He started swearing and, like his tough-looking friends, always spoke derogatorily of gay people.

And then, Kanye West's view of homosexuals changed. In a hurry. Life deals everyone a unique set of cards. Anything brought closer to home becomes real. For example, cancer is a bad thing, a sad thing, until it invades your own family—and then it becomes a tragedy, something with a texture and sight and sounds and smells all its own. Once it is in your life, you understand it better. Tornadoes are from the Wizard of Oz, or something only those in Tornado Alley experience, until you have a tornado hit your town, and then it is something that shakes your world and gives you nightmares, giving it a meaning it never would have had if hadn't ever touched you personally. Watching on the news as people lose their houses to foreclosure looks like a pretty bad deal, but you still have your warm bed to go to and your TV on your dresser. Only when you are told your house is being taken out from underneath you can you honestly say you have walked in those people's shoes—right out the door, into the cruel world.

That's what happened to Kanye West. It turned out that one of Kanye's favorite cousins was gay. West felt horrible for his views and words toward and about gays. He loved his cousin and hated to think of the way people treated the young gay man—and Kanye hated the way he himself had spoken of gay people.

West said that he recognized right away that hip-hop had no tolerance for gays and lesbians, from the way women are portrayed in videos to the lyrics in songs. He heard people describe bad songs by calling the song gay. West said the word with the opposite meaning of the word "hip-hop" is the word "gay."

Coming out in support of tolerance cost West one of his friends. It turns out one of West's friends used to wear a *College Dropout* T-shirt, but after West expressed his thoughts on hip-hop's degradation of gays, his friend announced that he would no longer wear the shirt. West said he was content to speak from his own heart and let his friend make that decision. West said he would rather put himself in the crosshairs of criticism while standing up for any civil right than stand silent and watch persecution that he believes is wrong.

Kanye was asked if he would take up the cause of getting degrading comments and terms about women out of the rap community. West said that was not his particular cause, that he thought gay-bashing was more prevalent than negativity toward women. Although women are called nasty names in songs, West said, he is more troubled by how gays are called hateful names to their faces. The issue hit home when he was with a former girlfriend out shopping, and Kanye himself used the word "fag." It turned out there were a few gay people in the store he and his former girlfriend were shopping in at the time, and she was offended, telling Kanye to "step into the new millennium."[10] He also said talking about gay people and preaching tolerance was very costly to him in the rap community, but that he was comfortable because he knew he was right in advocating for gays to be treated with respect.

"I got more backlash for that than for the Bush comment," West said. "It's wrong, and so many of my friends do that. We gay-bash. We feel like it's OK to call a gay person a fag. We fought so hard to make it so white people couldn't say the word 'nigger' to our face. But it's not far-fetched to picture a black person calling a gay person a fag to their face. So that shows you the climate, where we're at right now. And it's not about racism, it's about discrimination."[11]

Kanye West is sensitive to the civil rights of everyone. And from his family's roots in Oklahoma City, it is easy to understand why. Many of Kanye and his mother's summer or holiday trips took them from Chicago to their family in Oklahoma. Kanye's civil rights lineage goes way back, at least as far as his grandfather, Portwood Williams Sr. When Donda West was a little girl in Oklahoma City, her father, a rights activist, took his children to sit-ins as a form of protest against racism in the late 1950s. Donda went with her father to one such event at Katz Drugstore in Oklahoma City in 1958. Donda West said in September 2007 that her son should speak up any time he is so moved.

"I do think that Kanye is a voice that can definitely be used and should be used not only in hip-hop but across the arts, period," Donda said. "I think he is broader than a genre. I think he has a calling to reach a number of people. Kanye keeps it real. He touches the people. You never know how words can save a person's life, physically or otherwise. People like Martin Luther King or Mahatma Gandhi or, in my view, Barack Obama, or Jesus Christ—people whose job it is to tell the truth—I see that in Kanye. Now, people like you are going to go, 'Oh, Kanye's mom said he's like Jesus!' But when you have a gift, you didn't get it by yourself. Your truth is your truth."[12]

Kanye's grandfather Portwood, Donda's father, remains a man of strong beliefs and conviction and is regarded in the community as someone who has affected the lives of a lot of young people in a very positive way. According to comments in an Oklahoma City newspaper article, Portwood has a unique combination of humor and leadership, so much so that many regarded him as the "Bill Cosby of Oklahoma City," according to the newspaper story.[13]

Oklahoma has a history with civil rights, and some of it involves the country's darkest hours. The Tulsa Race Riot, or Greenwood Riot, happened between May 31 and June 1, 1921. A 19-year-old black man stepped into an elevator, and a woman operating it screamed. Stories vary on what happened next. One says the man, Dick Rowland, a shoe shiner who was getting into the elevator to take it to the top floor where the restroom for "coloreds" was, accidentally stepped on her foot, knocking her off balance, and reached out to grab her—which allegedly caused her to scream, and caused Rowland to flee. Another version said he was assaulting her, hard to imagine in a crowded building in a public elevator. Regardless, Rowland was arrested for sexual assault, though Sarah Page never gave a formal statement to police, and no manhunt was enacted after police were called. Parts of the white community wanted a lynching, and the *Tulsa Tribune* had a headline that read, "To Lynch Negro Tonight"; the black community wanted to protect Rowland, recalling that just one year earlier, in 1920, a Jewish boy had been lynched by a white mob in Tulsa as police directed traffic around the group.

Rumors flew all day about what was happening. But this much is certain: Outside the courthouse, 75 armed black men told the sheriff they could protect Rowland, though he refused. A black World War I veteran, wearing his uniform and holding his military-issued service revolver, was accosted by a white man. That gun or another discharged, and racial riots started. Whites fired at the black men, who retreated to Greenwood, though several blacks lay dead in the street before they could retreat. Whites chased the blacks, and in Greenwood, whites set fire to black businesses, and as Tulsa Fire Department trucks showed up to put the blazes out, they were turned away at gunpoint by whites. According to witnesses, six World War I–era biplanes were used to drop incendiary bombs on blacks in Tulsa, though whites claimed they were being used to help police with surveillance.

Media reports differ on how many were killed, as white militia members were rumored to have killed as many as 3,000 blacks. The Red Cross said the number was at least 300, but the official death toll from white public officials was 29 blacks killed and 10 whites. Over the course of 16 hours of rioting through the night, 35 city blocks were burned in the largely black neighborhood of Greenwood. Eight-hundred were admitted to hospitals, and 10,000 were left homeless. Mass graves were dug by blacks, which could have led to an underreporting of death tolls. Greenwood had been a beacon of black prosperity, with the Greenwood area being called "The Negro Wall Street."

The Ku Klux Klan came to Tulsa in August of that year to peddle its brand of hate. Oklahoma, from its statehood in 1907 to the riots in 1921, had had 26 known lynchings of blacks.

Oklahoma City, though, became part of America—and the world's— conscience when it became—at the time—the site of the worst terrorist attack on American soil.

Kanye West's grandfather is, and was in 1995, a proud resident of Oklahoma City. A bomb taking up the entire back of a rental truck was detonated, and it blew off the whole front of the Murrah Federal Building in Oklahoma City on April 19, 1995. What was left standing looked like the back wall of a dollhouse, so powerful and deadly was the explosion. News reports had the government developing lists of known Middle Eastern terrorists, some of whom were tied to the 1991 World Trade Center bombings. But this time, the attack was committed by an American. Former U.S. Army soldier Timothy McVeigh, a veteran of the first Gulf War, was a sympathizer to white militias that had been attacked by the U.S. government in Ruby Ridge, Idaho, and to a well-armed, self-proclaimed prophet's cult compound in Waco, Texas. Both the Idaho and Texas raids were carried out clumsily and in deadly fashion by agents from the Bureau of Alcohol, Tobacco and Firearms, and in the case of the Waco massacre, the timing was such that television news crews could come along and film it—though that backfired because the cult was tipped off. The Oklahoma City bombing happened on the two-year anniversary of the Waco raid.

It was this political backdrop that Timothy McVeigh claimed justified his slaughter of 168 people working at a government building in Oklahoma City, including six children, the youngest a three-month-old. President Bill Clinton called the bombing an "act of cowardice" and "evil."

A very alert Oklahoma state trooper, Charlie Hanger, noticed a car without license plates, found a weapon in the car, and arrested 26-year-old Timothy McVeigh. Another Army veteran, Terry Nichols, was convicted along with McVeigh. Although McVeigh was unapologetic when his death sentence was carried out—he even mapped out his escape route and contributed to a book about the bombing, calling the children killed "collateral" damage—Nichols is serving life without parole in prison.

NOTES

1. *OK! Magazine.* "Mike Myers Credits Oprah for Love Guru." June 18, 2008.

2. Terry Moran. "Home with Kanye West." *Nightline*, ABC News, September 24, 2007.

3. Nui Te Koha. "Kanye's New Sort of Rap." *(Australia) Sunday Mail*, September 16, 2007.

4. Katy O'Donnell. "Kanye West's Mother on Parenting and More." *Baltimore Sun* blogs, September 2007, http://weblogs.baltimoresun.com/entertainment/critics/blog/2007/09/kanye_wests_mother_on_parentin.html.

5. Austin Skaggs. "Troublemaker of the Year." *Rolling Stone*, December 15, 2005.

6. Jan M. Olsen. "Kanye West Sore Loser at MTV Europe Awards." Associated Press, November 3, 2006.

7. Ellen DeGeneres. "Interview with Kanye West." *The Ellen DeGeneres Show*, September 14, 2007.

8. Ibid.

9. Terry Moran. "Home with Kanye West."

10. Belazon.com. December 20, 2007, http://www.bellazon.com/main/index.php?showtopic=12758.

11. Sway Calloway. "All Eyes on Kanye West." MTV.com, August 18, 2005.

12. Katy O'Donnell. "Kanye West's Mother on Parenting and More."

13. George Lang. "Rap Star's Mom Left a Legacy." *The Oklahoman*, November 20, 2007.

Chapter 12

2007–2008: A PERIOD OF BIG WINS AND DEEP LOSSES

Donda West had long established her place in this world before she left it prematurely.

On November 10, 2007, at age 58, Donda passed away from what were deemed postsurgical complications related to anesthesia—used to put people out for operations.[1]

A three-decade career in education, culminating as chair of the English department at Chicago State University, established Dr. West as a scholar and academic with remarkable credentials. She taught thousands of students through the years, shaping their lives and helping them develop the kind of love and understanding of the language that she lived by and inspired in her own son as well.

The list of those at her memorial service in 2007 showed how many she had touched. In addition to Jay-Z, Beyoncé Knowles, and others of fame—Anita Baker was accompanied by up-and-coming artist Legend in performing one of Donda's favorite songs, "Summertime"—most in attendance were people who had simply been lucky enough to have Donda West as a teacher, coworker, mentor, or friend.

Though she had retired to serve as Kanye's manager, Donda West still made time for those whom she had always found time to shape and help, and just months before her passing she had gone back to Chicago State University to deliver the keynote at a major writers' conference.

Her students remember being told the first day of class that no question they asked would be stupid and that any knowledge she had would be shared with whoever wanted to learn it. Ironically, she served in an administrative position as chairperson, but she always preferred guiding students rather than dealing with academic bureaucracy, paperwork, and policies.

When she moved Kanye at age three to Chicago, she started working at Chicago State and made what she considered a king's ransom of $17,000 a year, a $10,000 per year increase over what she had been making at Morris Brown. She utilized all of higher education's resources to the fullest, teaching in China for a year.

In the year leading up to her death, Donda had remarked that what she was looking forward to most was the day Kanye would marry and start giving her grandchildren to dote on.

Donda West had decided, on her own, to have plastic surgery in November 2007. Kanye had always told his mother that she looked great but that she could make her own decisions and could certainly do as she chose. She had a good year and a good summer, going to her 40th high school reunion, where she donated several copies of her new book, signed by both her and Kanye, to be used as a fundraiser in a silent auction.[2]

Donda grew up with the affectionate nickname "Big Girl" from her father.[3] It was not a negative term and in fact was a term of endearment. Donda embraced the name and even signed cards to her father with that. She certainly was not big, either. No, she was not skin and bones or model thin, but that is often less healthy than carrying a few extra pounds, as a majority of Americans do.

While teaching college, it is hard to imagine Donda would have had the means or the money to have plastic surgery, especially from the plastic surgeon she chose. Dr. Jan Adams, a sort of celebrity doctor in Beverly Hills, was, like Dr. Phil, more noted for his television work promoting his craft than he was for his surgical skills. He had a British television program and a Discovery Health show, *Plastic Surgery, Before & After*, and also served as a co-host on a show that was supposed to be the male version of the popular and often controversial Barbara Walters–produced show *The View*.

Dr. Adams wrote a book for major U.S. publisher St. Martin's titled *Everything Women of Color Should Know about Plastic Surgery*. Dr. Adams was also a guest of the world's most popular talk-show host, Oprah Winfrey. It was never mentioned in the book or in these television interviews—or even in major media—that in 2001 Dr. Adams had reached six-figure settlements in two malpractice suits that had earlier been filed against him. He also had multiple driving-under-the-influence charges brought against him, which he took responsibility for later in a television interview.

It is hard to say if age or a preexisting condition made Donda, at age 58, an unsuitable candidate to have the two procedures done by Dr. Adams.

According to an ABC *Nightline* program that aired shortly after her death, Donda had both a tummy tuck and a breast reduction surgery, two significant procedures that taxed her body. She obviously was under anesthesia for the operations. She was resting the next day when paramedics were called to her Los Angeles home and were unable to revive her. Some 200-plus people die from plastic surgery complications each year.

But at least one doctor Donda consulted with before the surgery, Andre Aboolian, warned her that having such plastic surgery would be risky for her and insisted she get medical clearance from another doctor. When she called Aboolian back to say she still wanted to have him perform the surgery, she admitted she had not gotten medical clearance, so he said he would not perform the procedure.

"I always insist on a medical clearance for women over 40, and in this instance it was particularly important because of a condition she had that I felt could have led to a heart attack," Aboolian said in a statement released to CNN. Another doctor, Renato Calabria, told MTV News that he requires anyone close to 60 years old who is overweight to be medically tested and cleared before he will perform plastic surgery on them.

Donda went to Dr. Jan Adams at that point, and he agreed to perform the surgery, but she stopped breathing at her home after being released following the surgery. All doctors interviewed for MTV's November 13, 2007, article on the death said they would have not performed the surgery unless Dr. West had had her heart tested and was medically cleared. All doctors interviewed also said it was a poor decision to send or let her go home so soon after the surgery, and she should have been kept at a hospital or some sort of health care facility after the surgery. Though she did have the right to choose to go home—an option obviously exercised—doctors could require, pre-surgery, that the patient agree to an outpatient facility or hospital for aftercare.

In 2008, a more thorough and final autopsy report was issued, stating that Donda West had coronary artery disease—something that likely would have been detected and treated with pre-surgery testing ordered by other doctors, but not Dr. Jan Adams—and "various complications from plastic surgery." She had a cardiac event—likely a heart attack—and stopped breathing and was alone at the time, though friends were downstairs, and one of them is who found Donda not breathing that evening.[4]

Donda had accomplished a lot in her life and had taken steps in her own career in 2007. She wrote a book about raising Kanye and what it was like growing up as a single mother and how she enjoyed teaching college English. No one was prouder of her than her son, who wrote the song "Hey Mama" as a tribute to her, saying how proud he was of her. She had retired early from Chicago State University as chair of the English department to help manage Kanye's career, running his foundation and managing his new venture, West Brands, LLC.

Kanye felt compassion from around the world, including from someone who had been his biggest rival just months earlier, 50 Cent.

"I can definitely understand how that's a huge loss, and how that would be, and his relationship with his mom had a lot more depth to it than a lot of people's," 50 Cent told the Associated Press 10 days after Kanye's mother died. "He was real close to his mom. I hope that he can work his way through it. If you're active, you'll find reasons to smile, reasons to be happy."[5]

Kanye's acceptance speech at the Grammys for best rap album in February 2008 was classic Kanye. Though he would go on to win a total of four Grammys that night, his speech, along with a special performance of "Hey Mama"—he had Mama shaved into his head—made it memorable. His speech for rap album follows:[6]

> "It definitely feels good to be home here at the Grammys," West started. "You know, we snuck in about four years ago, four or five years ago and now we basically made this our new place of residence. Working on a hip-hop album, and the state of the music game—they say, like, you know, you can't sell records. A lot of people said hip-hop was dead—not just Nas, but, you know, a lot of people just said the art form wasn't popping like that anymore. I wanted to cross the genres and show people, you know, how we could still express ourselves with something fresh and new and that's what hip-hops always been about, you know, coming out with new sounds and stuff."

He smiled and addressed his competitors.

"You got to time the album better, you can't drop them the same year as me, this is my award," West said.[7]

Music in the background started, trying to get Kanye to finish and get off the stage, a common though annoying practice at such shows, including the Academy Awards and the Emmys.

"Come on—you going to play music on me?" West asked. He continued, over the music, addressing artist Amy Winehouse and her producer, Mark Ronson. "For Mark Ronson and Amy Winehouse, if I don't get to get up here for album of the year, you deserve it just as much as me—I deserve it, too."[8]

He turned serious, even though the background music would not abate.

"Just to say something about my mother: I appreciate all the support, I appreciate all the prayers," West said.

The music got louder, and Kanye took the unusual step of telling the producers that this moment was one he—and they—would never have again, and there was something he simply had to say.

"It would be in good taste to stop the music," West said. The music stopped, and the crowd loudly applauded. He finished by addressing his mother specifically, who had passed away the previous October. "I appreciate everything, and I know you are really proud of me right now. And I know you wouldn't want me to stop, and you want me to be the number one artist in the world. And Mama, all I'm gonna do is keep making you proud. We run this."[9]

HIGHS AND LOWS

The theme of triumph and tragedy ran back to back throughout 2007 and 2008 for Kanye.

Evel Knievel was a shrewd self-marketer, creating his own brand by taking something that had been done—jumping motorcycles—and taking it to a whole new level.

He was a rebel, literally an outlaw, and he made crowds "ooh" and "ahh" like they never did for anyone else. Knievel, from the rough-and-tumble mining town of Butte, Montana, had been a standout hockey player in high school. After measuring himself in an East Coast semi-pro league as not being able to make it to the National Hockey League, Knievel decided to start jumping motorcycles. He was no stranger to the cycle—he had stolen his first Harley Davidson when he was 13. But at age 27 in Moses Lake, Washington, Knievel bought half-interest in a motorcycle shop. To get the store attention, he planned to jump his cycle over parked cars, a tethered mountain lion, and a box of rattlesnakes. He cleared everything—except the snakes. He said he knew he could draw a crowd by jumping his cycle over "weird stuff."

In 1965 he formed a motorcycle group that toured the nation doing jumps. He broke off onto his own in 1968, and the legend was formally born. In 1968 he tried to jump the fountains at Caesars Palace in Las Vegas. It did not go well. A fractured skull, broken pelvis, and broken hip and ribs were the first of the estimated 433 bones he would break in his jumping career. Knievel jumped everything in sight, and even when he cleared the distance, the landing was not always smooth, with the bike careening out of control and Knievel getting nothing but more broken bones—and more fans. And more money.

Toys were made depicting Evel Knievel on his motorcycle, with his cape flying and wearing his stars-and-striped jumpsuit and helmet, and they flew off the shelves and brought in millions of dollars. He jumped a shark tank in Chicago and broke his left collarbone and right arm. Knievel was the bread-and-butter, the most watched attraction, on ABC's *Wide World of Sports*. Thousands would show up, and millions would tune in to watch the daredevil do things in ways no one had done them before, and certainly no one had done them Knievel's bravado and confidence.

He wanted to jump the Grand Canyon in Arizona, but the U.S. government shut that idea down. The Department of the Interior was not about to pick up pieces of his proposed jet-powered motorcycle—and pieces of Knievel himself in all likelihood—off the floor of the canyon.

So Knievel bought a nice little chunk on the scenic Snake River Canyon in Idaho. In 1974, he was launched from something that looked like it was supposed to send a rocket into outer space. He fired off into the air with millions watching—and $6 million in his pocket for the event—and touched the sky. But he didn't clear the gorge; the rocket's parachute deployed in mid-flight. He dropped sadly and slowly into the canyon, where he was rescued, with only some cuts on his face. Knievel claimed the parachute malfunctioned and opened on its own.

That image, of the rocket soaring into the air, was etched in a lot of baby boomers' minds when Kanye West became "Kanye Kanyevel" for his video for "Touch the Sky." The elaborate production, which included *Baywatch* star Pamela Anderson and a host of others, was a reenactment of Knievel's most famous moment in time.

The video was a smash success on MTV and was among the more celebrated videos of the year. Kanye West was certainly proud of it.

But in Florida, Even Knievel, dealing with, among other issues, hepatitis, a liver transplant, and the aches and pain that came with being the world's most high-profile daredevil ever, was not laughing.

Knievel, whose real name was Robert Craig Knievel, filed suit in federal court on Monday, December 12, 2006, claiming West used Knievel's likeness and trademarked name. He called the images of a scantily clad Anderson vulgar and offensive and said the video damaged his reputation.[10]

"That video that Kanye West put out is the most worthless piece of crap I've ever seen in my life, and he uses my image to catapult himself on the public," the 68-year-old Knievel said.[11] The lawsuit, which includes a cover of a 1974 *Sports Illustrated* to show the visual similarities between Knievel's actual jump and West's video, wanted both damages and to cease distribution of the video.

Of course, Knievel had admitted to misbehavior that Kanye West has never been near in his life. Knievel bragged of his sexual exploits, beat a former colleague with a baseball bat, and was considered by many to be, well, rather offensive and vulgar. West's lawyers claimed that Knievel was such an iconic figure that the image was part of the public domain and thus allowed to be used for artistic purposes, even parody. The two sides agreed to mediation, and the case was on hold.

Knievel's health was deteriorating rapidly. He was a shell of his former self, and he knew it. When Donda West died suddenly after cosmetic surgery, Knievel invited Kanye into his home to settle the matter. Knievel could not have been impressed more. Kanye had never meant to damage Knievel's reputation and was in fact paying homage to Knievel's incredible showmanship and entrepreneurial spirit, qualities West as an entertainer certainly shares.

In November of 2007, just weeks after his mother's death, Kanye West and Evel Knievel became friends and settled their differences.

"I thought he was a wonderful guy and quite a gentleman," Knievel said.[12]

Knievel was so impressed with West that they took a picture together, a trend-setter with an unmistakable brand from decades earlier standing with a modern-day icon and risk taker who was setting his own trends and creating his own brand, a brand even more far-reaching and lucrative than Knievel's. The motorcycle legend said he felt for Kanye and hoped he could get through the pain of his mother's death.

"I know he's had some tough times the past few weeks," Knievel said, "and I hope things work out."[13]

The settlement was never made public. And not more than a week after burying the hatchet with Kanye West, Robert Craig "Evel" Knievel died on November 30, 2007, at age 69, hopefully touching the sky a final time and leaving the world at peace with Kanye West and, hopefully, himself.

In late July 2008, Kanye West did something that changed the lives of three U.S. military members who are war veterans. The three soldiers, two men and a woman, came home to financial woes, self-doubt, and post-traumatic stress. They were, as West noted, falling through the system's cracks, unable to make ends meet, and were on the verge of giving up their dreams of college educations, remaining in their homes, getting out from under debts, and even sending their own kids to college. Kanye had suffered the loss of his mother, the then-recent breakup with his longtime girlfriend and fiancée, and his often strained relationship with his father.

He and MTV's Sway Calloway surprised the veterans with a visit and with money from MTV and the foundation Kanye set up to honor his mother.

"I know my music inspires people, but you can always do more," West said after greeting the overwhelmed and grateful veterans and giving them tools to better their lives. He told them on the show, "You make me want to improve myself; we thought I'd come in and be an inspiration to you and lift your spirits, but actually you're inspirational to me because I'm going through a lot of losses."[14]

With a rough span behind him in 2008, Kanye West looked forward to a future of more music, more awards, and hopefully, a lot more happiness.

NOTES

1. Jacob Adelman. "Rapper Kanye West's Mother Dies." Associated Press, November 11, 2007, http://www.gbmnews.com/articles/1937/1/Rapper-Kanye-Wests-Mother-Dies/Page1.html.

2. George Lang. "Rap Star's Mom Left a Legacy." *The Oklahoman*, November 20, 2007.

3. Donda West. *Raising Kanye: Life Lessons from the Mother of a Hip-Hop Superstar*. New York: Pocket Books, 2007.

4. *The Smoking Gun*. "Donda West Autopsy Release." January 10, 2008.

5. Nekesa Mumbi Moody. "50 Cent Offers Condolences to Kanye West, Says Good to Keep Performing Despite Grief." Associated Press Worldstream, November 21, 2007.

6. Jake Coyle. "Kanye West Honors His Deceased Mother by Singing Special Version of 'Hey Mama' at Grammys." Associated Press, February 11, 2008.

7. Kanye West. "2008 Grammy Acceptance Speech." Onsmash.com, February 11, 2008, http://videos.onsmash.com/v/NejCebiXqZw148J2.

8. Ibid.

9. Ibid.

10. Mitch Stacy. "Daredevil Knievel Sues Rapper Kanye West over Video." Associated Press, December 12, 2006.

11. Ibid.

12. Associated Press. "Evel Knievel, Kanye West Settle Lawsuit." November 28, 2007.

13. Ibid.

14. Jocelyn Vena. "Kanye West and MTV Hear Veterans' Stories—and Help Them—in 'Homecoming.'" MTV.com, July 28, 2008.

Appendix A

JUNE 8, A NOTABLE DAY IN HISTORY

Certainly, with only 365 days in a year and thousands of events going on that have shaped the world in which we live, each date will have something significant to almost any person, anywhere.

Kanye West was born on June 8, 1977, and for those who are into looking at just how the stars were aligned on that day, there is a lot to consider when the date of June 8 is examined through recent and long-ago history.

The date is wrought particularly with natural disasters. On June 8, 1783, Iceland's Laki volcano began a violent eruption that lasted eight months, killing some 9,000 people and starting a famine that lasted another seven years.

In terms of relating to Kanye's deep belief and commitment to civil rights, as he showed with his Hurricane Katrina volunteer work and donations, and support of other such movements, on June 8, 1789, Congressman James Madison proposed a Bill of Rights to Congress. As the main writer, he was considered the "father" of the Constitution and was responsible for the first 10 Amendments to the Constitution, many of which focused on rights and freedoms. Madison of course would go onto become a two-term president after serving as President Thomas Jefferson's secretary of state, and supervised the logistics of the Louisiana Purchase.

Additionally, on the date June 8, 632, the Prophet Muhammad died. Andrew Jackson, the seventh U.S. president, died on June 8, 1845, in Tennessee.

Years later, on June 8, 1861, Tennessee was the 11th and last state to secede from the Union in the American Civil War, which of course would ultimately free slaves. In international conflict, the date also comes up. On June 8, 1941, the Allies invaded Syria and Lebanon, and on June 8, 1942, Japanese submarines shelled two major Australian cities. On Kanye West's sixth birthday, June 8, 1983, Negro League baseball legend Satchell Paige passed away.

Entertainment also stakes a claim to significant events on the date. On June 8, 1948, one of the most long-lasting comedians in history, Milton Berle, hosted the debut of the Texaco Star Theater. Just one year later on June 8, 1949, it was a dark day for America as the FBI, seeking to attach the label of "Communist" to anyone it thought subversive, named Helen Keller, Danny Kaye, and other educators and celebrities as Communists in an official FBI report.

In addition to Madison's Bill of Rights and the effort of the FBI to deny Kaye and Keller civil rights, there are several other significant events on the date related to civil rights. On June 8, 1968, James Earl Ray was arrested for the murder of Martin Luther King Jr., arguably the most important civil rights crusader not just in America, but perhaps the world. On that exact same day, the body of murdered U.S. Senator, and former U.S. Attorney General, Robert F. Kennedy was buried in Arlington.

Another U.S. natural disaster fell June 8, 1974, when Emporia, Kansas, was hit by an F-4 tornado, killing six people.

Kanye shares his June 8 birthday with such people as comedienne Joan Rivers, actor Keenan Ivory Wayans, Duran Duran's Nick Rhodes, and singer Nancy Sinatra, daughter of music legend Frank Sinatra.

Appendix B

AWARDS AND SONGS

American Music Awards:

2004: no wins, three nominations. Favorite Breakthrough Artist, Favorite Rap-Hip-Hop Artist, and Favorite Rap/Hip-Hop Album.

2006: no wins, two nominations. Favorite Pop/Rock Male Artist and Favorite Rap/Hip-Hop Male Artists.

Grammy Awards/Nominations:

2005: nine nominations, three wins.

Nominations: Album of the Year (*The College Dropout*), Song of the Year ("Jesus Walks"), Best New Artist, Best Rap Solo Performance ("Through the Wire"), Best Rap/Sung Collaboration ("All Falls Down"), Best Rap/Sung Collaboration ("Slow Jamz").

Wins: Best R&B Song ("You Don't Know My Name)," Best Rap Song ("Jesus Walks"), and Best Rap Album (*The College Dropout*).

2006: seven nominations, three wins.

Nominations: Album of the Year (*Late Registration*), Record of the Year ("Gold Digger"), Best R&B Song ("Unbreakable"), Best Rap/Sung Collaboration ("They Say").

Wins: Best Rap/Solo Performance ("Gold Digger"), Best Rap Song ("Diamonds from Sierra Leone"), Best Rap Album (*Late Registration*).

2008: eight nominations, four wins.

Nominations: Album of the Year (*Graduation*), Best Rap Performance by a Duo or Group ("Classic [Better Than I've Ever Seen]"), Best Rap/Sung Collaboration ("Good Life"), Best Rap Song ("Can't Tell Me Nothing").

Wins: Best Rap Solo Performance ("Stronger"), Best Rap Performance by a Duo or Group ("South Side"), Best Rap Song ("Good Life"), and Best Rap Album (*Graduation*).

SONGS

Kanye West's lyrics are, for the most part, autobiographical sketches of where he has been, where he is, and where he is headed. He celebrates his successes, points out those who doubt him, pays tribute to those he cares about, and often uses his sense of humor. Here is a short look and one person's interpretations of most of the songs from West's three CDs.

The College Dropout, released February 10, 2004. Songs include the following:

"We Don't Care": A song about how the drug business and drug problems would supposedly reduce the life span of African American males to 25 years and about how enterprising blacks were often written off by the system but went on to make good wages. The hook that keeps repeating is that they do not care what other people say about them.

"Graduation Day": About how Kanye's graduation into success in the real world did not include the formal education and college degree that is does for most young people.

"All Falls Down": Starts out as a tribute to Chicago, particularly Kanye's native South Side. The song talks about how a young woman is staying in college even though the subject she is majoring in does not produce high-paying jobs, but she stays in school regardless because of peer pressure. Has a classic line about naming her child "Alexis" because she can't afford to buy a "Lexus." Has another line about how money can get someone out of jail but cannot buy them real freedom.

"I'll Fly Away": Though it did not get the attention of "Jesus Walks," this is a very spiritual song, with several references to "O, Glory" and "Hallelujah" and how when he dies, he will fly away to what God has waiting for him.

"Spaceship": A song about working in a store for a manager who shows no appreciation for the worker, and the worker just wants to get off the graveyard shift but does not make enough money to chase his dreams, so he wishes he could buy a spaceship. Includes lyrics about people being negative and doubting him. Ends with him making it as a star but still not having enough money for the spaceship, so he will keep on working.

"Jesus Walks": A very powerful song, not just for its reference to Jesus, but for the social causes it address. The chorus is about how God's soldiers are at war with terrorism, racism, and society, but the war looming over it all is the one with ourselves. He is afraid he has not prayed in so long that God might not listen, and he hopes he can walk, like Jesus, to salvation.

"Never Let Me Down": A song with a hard edge. Talks about how he told his grandmother he would never let her down. He pays tribute his grandfather for taking his mother, Donda, to sit-ins in Oklahoma City in the late 1950s, which were used for civil rights protest while the country was in the throes of racism.

"The New Workout Plan": Rhyme and rhythm about working out, starting with abdominal training. Also in the chorus he talks about a guy and his girlfriend working out problems in their relationship. Female guest vocalists rap about how "Kanye's workout" tape made their lives better.

"Through the Wire": Literally recorded while his jaw was wired shut from a car accident he was at fault for. He raps about eating through a straw, how his mom had to deal with knowing her son was in surgery while she was a thousand miles away before she could get to California to be by his side—and how he was treated in the same hospital where Biggie Smalls died after being shot. Also notes how wearing a seat belt saved his life. "He came up with a healthy respect for God, but the accident had a profound impact on him," Donda West told the *Chicago Tribune*. "He particularly knows that by the grace of God he was spared, and spared for a particular purpose. I've never witnessed him as a card-carrying Christian, he's just too hip-hop for that. But I think he has an appreciation for the fact that he could have been dead, and he feels there are angels watching him and protecting him."

"Breathe In Breathe Out": Makes fun of himself for claiming to change rap with his backpack and fashion sense, yet still raps about money, women, and how much money he had already blown getting stuff he really didn't need. Another reference to dropping out of school, something that appears in several tracks on this album in addition to the album title.

"School Spirit": Starts out with a list of common Greek names for fraternities and sororities that come from the Greek alphabet, such as Alpha, Sigma, Omega, Delta, Zeta, and so on. He raps about how he finished school—but how finishing for him did not include graduating—and about how one of his friends who did graduate was working as a waiter.

"Family Business": A tune about how his success has changed the interaction of family members, how certain people might have doubted him but now have memories he would rather they not share, and even how some would not eat a certain aunt's dishes at family gatherings. But he points out later in the song that he has no plans to let others in on family business.

"Last Call": He raps about how everyone expected that he would, as a college dropout, not succeed in life, but that all who doubted him can see him atop the hip-hop world and its charts. Talks in back-to-back sentences about first being overlooked and now being overlooked. Also raps about how No I.D. helped him get signed, about how he wanted to be not just a producer but a recording artist as well.

Notable: Won Grammy as Best Rap Album; single "Jesus Walks" won Grammy for Best Rap Song; Ranked number 1 in *Spin* magazine's top 40 albums; Album of the Year from *Rolling Stone* magazine.

Late Registration, released August 30, 2005. Songs include the following:

"Wake Up, Mr. West": Features the late Bernie Mac starting off with Bernie's unforgettable laugh. Recalls Kanye being told to behave in school and how "Mr. West" falls asleep in class.

"Heard 'Em Say": Guest appearing on this song is Adam Levine of Maroon 5. Blames the government for having "administered AIDS" on the black public and raps about how other social ills, such as legalized gambling in the form of lottery tickets, were designed to give blacks false hopes—and take more of their money in the process.

"Touch the Sky": The song that inspired an Evel Knievel–like video (and lawsuit). His not winning video of the year at the

Video Music Awards show in August for this song resulted in
his rant on stage. The song is autobiographical about how he
showed up at Roc-A-Fella records and was seen as being out of
place in his polo shirt. This song demonstrates West's uncanny
ability to rhyme words that do not actually rhyme whatsoever,
such as "them" and "apartment," or later "beats" and "KFC."
Talks about how all the wrongs he mentions throughout "Touch
the Sky" actually helped him write the song, so in the end the
wrongs had great value.

"Gold Digger": This is the song that Kanye brags about the most
and the one he seems to be most proud of, especially when he
expresses how various awards show did not recognize that "Gold
Digger" should have been a hands-down winner for song of the
year. The song, as told by its title, includes reference to spouses
who end up better off financially than the rich person they married and how the person who earned the fortune should have
been more aware of someone looking to marry a rich person.

"Drive Slow": Another autobiographical song—as almost all of
West's songs are—this one reveals that a friend nicknamed
Kanye "K-Rock" so that kids would not mess with Kanye. Really,
though, the song is about driving slow in an awesome ride that
lures the attention young men want, don't want, and sometimes
don't need.

"My Way Home": Common is featured on this intense song, which
talks about home being a place filled with hate and pain, though
Kanye is not referring to his home. He appears more to be paint-
ing a picture of the hopelessness felt in impoverished and crime-
ridden neighborhoods and of how even the ones who make it
out—he specifically refers to Mike Tyson—end up on such a
high pedestal that the distance they fall from eventually wipes
them out completely.

"Crack Music": Blames the U.S. government for creating crack
and heroin to make blacks and other minorities get an addiction
they could never cure, so that it would wipe them out eventually, and remarks on how music about drugs and violence resulted.

"Roses": A tribute to his grandmother who was dying of an in-
curable disease in a hospital bed. He says that if she had more
money, she'd get the best medicine, like others who had the ill-
ness but who were able to live on for many years because they
had better treatment and medical care. Has a very touching line

about how instead of sending flowers, the family being there are the actual roses for his grandmother.

"Bring Me Down": Talks about how the breeding of hate has brought down a lot of powerful figures in the rap world and how people are trying to bring him down.

"Addiction": A song that did not get a lot of attention, it talks about how addiction can be drugs, money, or even the opposite sex.

"Diamonds from Sierra Leone": Though the song is noted for the "conflict diamonds" from Sierra Leone, it's also a song about how Kanye overcame his doubters and those who wonder if he and Jay-Z really get along now that Kanye is successful. The song is a tribute as well to how Roc-A-Fella records is still "alive and well."

"Hey Mama": A flat-out song of gratitude and love to his mother, about how proud he is of her, and how he promises he will return to school someday. Completely autobiographical, starting with when Donda moved her son with her to Chicago when he was three years old. A touching song that at the end talks about how he'll call his Mom any day; it does not have to be her birthday or Mother's Day.

Notable: Sold more than 3.5 million copies; *Rolling Stone* Album of the Year; Received the only five-star (highest possible) rating from *Rolling Stone*; Won 2006 Grammy for Best Rap Album.

Graduation, released September 11, 2008. Songs include the following:

"Good Morning": As was his theme for his first two albums, and as this one is titled, "Good Morning" is about graduation into the real world. He declares himself legendary and pronounces himself a better-dressed version of Malcolm X. He even raps about how others are more critical of him now that he has graduated to being a superstar.

"Champion": A thoughtful tribute to, and rebuke of, his father. He is grateful for the way his father provided for him in the summers, but talks about "hair-brained" get-rich plans and then launches into his own rise to the championship level of hip-hop star.

"Stronger": A powerful, inspirational chorus surrounded by verses that talk about who he is dating and his sense of style; it even refers to his well-publicized moniker of "Louis Vuitton Don."

"I Wonder": A song that talks about dreams throughout, specifically about how Kanye achieved all of his dreams and how he
worked so hard to make his dreams a reality.

"Good Life": Though he briefly refers to those critical of him, this
song is about how he has achieved a very good life and even references how onetime rival 50 Cent told him to develop his own
style no matter what anyone said and that the result would be
lots of money.

"Can't Tell Me Nothing": Includes several Christian references, but
asks questions about such as if a supreme being decides everything, just who decides the wars? He critiques himself for his
occasionally outlandish behavior, probably referring to at least
one awards show, but talks about how he has a lot of money but
hasn't changed and how his mother cautioned him on his
spending.

"Barry Bonds": Neither a baseball song nor really anything to do
with baseball homerun king Barry Bonds; rather, Kanye uses
Bonds as an analogy for Kanye's own string of hits. He compli-
ments himself for being a "better sport" in the past year.

"Flashing Lights": A song that goes all over the place, referring
to how at once his life has become very difficult, yet his life at
times seems like a series of flashing lights. He admits to being a
showman, but claims even the audience could not have imag-
ined he could have taken it all "this far."

"Everything I Am": Starts out by crediting fellow hip-hop artist
and Chicago native Common with passing him the song's beat.
Refers to several other artists, including Jay-Z's wife Beyoncé
Knowles. Includes a great line about how everything that he
isn't actually made him into all that he is. Says that although
some might think his 15 minutes are up, he's not done yet.

"The Glory": Uses the word "war" nine times in the chorus and
again continues the theme of fashion with references, like several of the other songs, to Louis Vuitton. He also refers to touring with Common. Says that he has no problem when he's gone
being compared to B.I.G.

"Homecoming": A classic tribute to his hometown of Chicago, aka
the Windy City. Talks about how entertainers from Chicago
leave to make it big. Features Chris Martin from Coldplay.

"Big Brother": This is one of the more memorable songs he has on
this album, a tribute to his "big brother" Jay-Z. The song refers
to how Kanye felt snubbed at a concert where artists he had

produced were performing, and rather than being up on stage singing a verse or even getting a backstage pass, he was offered only complimentary tickets out in the crowd. Also talks about Chicago rap legend No I.D., who was Kanye's first hip-hop mentor. Even pokes Jay-Z a bit for following Kanye's lead and using Coldplay for a song.

"Goodnight": Another song about dreaming and about living in the present and not focusing on the past. Mos Def does an amazing job with a moving chorus about saying good night, instead of saying good-bye.

"Bittersweet Poetry": Grammy winner John Mayer contributes to this song, which is about the ups and downs of a relationship gone bad and how relationships should not hurt so much.

Notable: *Graduation* won three Grammys, including the Grammy for Best Rap Album—for the third time in as many albums. Only Eminem has ever won three Grammys for Best Rap Album for his first three albums.

BIBLIOGRAPHY

MAGAZINE STORIES

Chappelle, Dave. "Hip-Hop on a Higher Level." *XXL*, September 2004.

Cohen, Edie. "Hip-Hop and Pop." *Interior Design*, August 2007.

Crosley, Hillary. "IKanyeClast." *Billboard*, August 11, 2007.

Davis, Kimberly. "Kanye West: Hip-Hop's New Big Shot." *Ebony*, April 2005.

Ecko, Mark. "Future Shock." *Complex*, August–September, 2007.

Foxx, Jamie. "Kanye West." *Interview* magazine, August 2004.

Friedman, Sarah A. "The Last Laugh." *Vibe*, July 2005.

Heckman, James, and Paul A. LaFontaine. "The Declining American High School Graduation Rate: Evidence, Sources, and Consequences." VOX, February 13, 2008.

Hits. "West Is Best." September 21, 2007.

Konigsberg, Eric. "Why Damon Dash Hates Mondays." *New York Magazine*, June 12, 2006.

McAlley, John. "Entertainer of the Year: Kanye West." *Spin*, December 20, 2007.

Norris, Chris. "Top of the World." *Blender*, September 2005.

Ogunnaike, Lola. "50 Cent: Taking Care of Business." *Rolling Stone*, September 20, 2007.

Ogunnaike, Lola. "West World." *Rolling Stone*, February 9, 2006

OK! *Magazine*. "Mike Myers Credits Oprah for Love Guru." June 18, 2008. Retrieved from http://www.okmagazine.com/news/view/7400.

Raymer, Alex. "Kanye West: Interview." *Timeout London*, September 14, 2005.

Raymer, Miles. "Come Home with Me." *XXL*, November 2007.

Rosen, Jody. "Way Out West." *Blender*, October 2007.

Skaggs, Austin. "Kanye: A Genius in Praise of Himself." *Rolling Stone*, September 20, 2007.

Skaggs, Austin. "Troublemaker of the Year." *Rolling Stone*, December 15, 2005.

Spencer, Amy. "A Fashionable Life." *Harper's Bazaar*, August 2007.

Tyrangiel, Josh. "Why You Can't Ignore Kanye." *Time*, August 21, 2005.

Valby, Karen. "The Ego Has Landed." *Entertainment Weekly*, February 3, 2006.

BOOKS

Clow, Kenneth, and Donald Blaack. *Integrated Advertising Promotion, and Marketing Communications*. Upper Saddle River, NJ: Pearson-Prentice Hall, 2007.

Jones, Charles Earl. *The Black Panther Party Reconsidered*. Baltimore, MD: Black Classic Press, 1998.

West, Donda. *Raising Kanye: Life Lessons from the Mother of a Hip-Hop Superstar*. New York: Pocket Books, 2007.

NEWSPAPERS

Bainbridge, Luke. "It's Kanye's World." *(London) Observer*, August 12, 2007.

Bream, Jon. "Kanye West: Is He Rap's Greatest Rock Star or Just Lost in Space?" *Minneapolis Star-Tribune*, June 10, 2008.

Cross, Hilary. "Live Nation, Jay-Z Deal Imminent." *Billboard*, April 2, 2008.

Daly, Sean. "Love or Hate Him. Doesn't Matter." *St. Petersburg Times*, May 1, 2008.

Eliscu, Jenny. "Genius Is as Genius Does." *USA Today Weekend*, August 19, 2007.

Koha, Nui Te. "Kanye's New Sort of Rap." *(Australia) Sunday Mail*, September 16, 2007.

Kot, Greg. "Rapper's Rise: From South Side to Top of the Charts." *Chicago Tribune*, February 11, 2004.

Lang, George. "Rap Star's Mom Left a Legacy." *The Oklahoman*, November 20, 2007. Retrieved from http://newsok.com/article/3171320/?print=1.

O'Donnell, Katy. "Kanye West's Mother on Parenting and More." *Baltimore Sun* blogs, September 2007. Retrieved from http://weblogs.baltimoresun.com/entertainment/critics/blog/2007/09/kanye_wests_mother_on_parentin.html.

Swift, Jacqui. "Perfectionist Rap Superstar on His Third Album." *The Sun (England)*, August 17, 2007.

Williams, John. "Kanye Wins Showdown." *Toronto Sun*, September 21, 2007.

NEWS SERVICES

Adelman, Jacob. "Rapper Kanye West's Mother Dies." Associated Press, November 11, 2007.

Associated Press. "After Losing at MTV's Video Music Awards, Kanye West Throws Another Tantrum." September 10, 2007.

Associated Press. "Evel Knievel, Kanye West Settle Lawsuit." November 28, 2007.

Associated Press. "Kanye West Blames MTV for Britney Spears' Lackluster Performance at the Video Music Awards." September 11, 2007.

Associated Press. "Kanye West Jams with Nas, John Legend." June 23, 2006.

Associated Press Worldstream. "Kanye West Says Justin Timberlake Is His 'Biggest Inspiration and Biggest Competition.'" August 21, 2007.

Coyle, Jake. "Kanye West Honors His Deceased Mother by Singing Special Version of 'Hey Mama' at Grammys." Associated Press, February 11, 2008.

Moody, Nekesa Mumbi. "50 Cent Offers Condolences to Kanye West, Says Good to Keep Performing Despite Grief." Associated Press Worldstream, November 21, 2007.

Olsen, Jan M.. "Kanye West Sore Loser at MTV Europe Awards." Associated Press, November 3, 2006.

Stacy, Mitch. "Daredevil Knievel Sues Rapper Kanye West over Video." Associated Press, December 12, 2006.

Tareen, Sophia. "Kanye West Voices Advocacy of Education in New Public-Service Announcement." Associated Press, August 24, 2007.

WEB PUBLICATIONS

Adaso, Henry. "A Brief History of Hip-Hop," June 25, 2008, http://rap.about.com/od/rootsofraphiphop/p/RootsOfRap.htm.

Angel. "Exclusive Backstage with Kanye West," May 9, 2008, http://concrete-loop.com/2008/05/exclusive-backstage-w-kanye-west.

Bartolomeo, Joey. "Kanye Spoofs Himself—But Blasts Critics," July 9, 2008, http://www.people.com/people/article/0,,20211262,00.html?xid=rss-fullcontentcnn.

BBC News. "50 Cent Will Quit if Sales Fail," August 11, 2007, http://news.bbc.co.uk/2/hi/entertainment/6942209.stm.

Calloway, Sway. "All Eyes on Kanye West," August 18, 2005, http://www.mtv.com/bands/w/west_kanye/news_feature_08180.

Moss, Corey. "Kanye West and John Mayer Collaborate But Won't Elaborate," November 18, 2004, http://www.mtvasia.com/News/200411/19008589.html.

Moss, Corey. "Kanye's at it Again," December 6, 2005, http://www.mtv.com/news/articles/1517545/20051206/west_kanye.jhtml?headlines=true.

Reid, Shaheem. "Kanye Recovering," October 22, 2002, http://www.mtv.com/news/articles/1458308/20021023/jay_z.jhtml.

Reid, Shaheem. "Kanye, Run-DMC, Outkast, Justin Sound Off on Our Top 10 Hip-Hop Groups," March 6, 2007, http://www.mtv.com/news/articles/1553911/20070305/west_kanye.jhtml.

The Smoking Gun. "Donda West Autopsy Release," January 10, 2008, http://www.thesmokinggun.com/archive/years/2008/0110083kanye1.html.

Vena, Jocelyn. "Kanye West and MTV Hear Veterans' Stories—and Help Them—in 'Homecoming,'" July 28, 2008, http://www.mtv.com/news/articles/1591708/20080728/west_kanye.jhtml.

Vozick-Levinson, Simon. "Jay-Z's Brotherly Love," Music Q&A. *Entertainment Weekly Online*, Fall 2007, http://www.ew.com/ew/article/0,,1567466_2001 0832_20057568,00.html.

RADIO INTERVIEWS

Brand, Madeline. "Hip-Hop Rivalry Has Roots in Rap Music," National Public Radio (NPR), September 11, 2007, http://www.npr.org/templates/story/story.php?storyId=14322398.

DJ Booth. "Kanye West Interview." DJBooth.net, September 3, 2007, http://www.djbooth.net/index/interviews/entry/kanye-west-interview-event-exclusive-0904071/.

VIDEO TV/INTERNET BROADCASTS

Banderas, Julie. "Interview with Donda West." *The Big Story with John Gibson*, FOX News, May 18, 2007.

DeGeneres, Ellen. "Interview with Kanye West." *The Ellen DeGeneres Show*, September 14, 2007, YouTube.com via http://www.TheCelebrityNewtwork.net.

Devore, Aeshia. "Kanye West Interview." *Teen Diaries TV*, October 9, 2007, http://www.youtube.com/watch?v=trM_bqBRuI0

BBC Radio. "'Graduation' album Q&A Session with Kanye West." 1XTra, London, England. Recorded at the BBC Radio Theatre, August 13, 2007, http://www.bbc.co.uk/1xtra/hiphop/kanye_day.shtml.

Moran, Terry. "Home with Kanye West." *Nightline*, ABC News, September 24, 2007.

Popworld. "Kanye West Interview." Channel 4, Great Britain, July 8, 2007, http://videos.onsmash.com/v/PSi8VkD2VjERChdD/

Rose, Charlie. "Interview with Jay-Z." PBS, November 9, 2007.

Sawyer, Diane, and Andrea Canning. "Plastic Surgery Nightmare: How Did Kanye's Mother Die?" *Good Morning America,* November 13, 2007.

West, Kanye. "2008 Grammy Acceptance Speech," Retrieved February 10, 2008 from YouTube.com via http://www.videosOnSmash.com,

HipHop-Elements.com. "Kanye West Interview." August 2007.

PR WEB SITES

Abrams, Neil. "Kanye West Launches New Online Travel Program." PR Newswire, March 31, 2008.

GOOD Music Label. http://www.GettingOutOurDreams.com. Owned by Kanye, the Web site features bios on each of the artists as well as information on how the label was formed.

James, Mike. "Business Runs on Water," March 7, 2007, http://www.blackenterprise.com/cms/exclusivesopen.aspx/id/2710.

Roc-A-Fella Records. Includes musical releases, artist information, and tour dates, http://www.Rocafella.com.

Kanye West's Web site. http://KanyeUniverseCity.com. Includes his blog, several news links, and merchandise.

West, Donda Clairann Williams. Dissertation abstract. Auburn University, 1980.

INDEX

About the Author

BOB SCHALLER completed his master's at Wyoming and his PhD at Texas Tech and teaches college writing at Stephen F. Austin State University in Texas. A former journalist, Schaller is the author of 40 books, including the children's series "X-Country Adventures," as well as several dozen biographies including *Never Stop Pushing* with Olympic wrestler Rulon Gardner, from Avalon; *Michael Phelps: The Untold Story of a Champion* from St. Martin's; and *The Complete Idiot's Guide to Running Injury-Free*.